Dragon **Naturally**Speaking®5

USER'S GUIDE

Lernout & Hauspie ™

DRAGON SYSTEMS

Contents

About This Guide

Welcome to Dragon NaturallySpeaking®, one of the world's most widely acclaimed speech-recognition products. Dragon NaturallySpeaking lets you talk to your computer instead of typing. It also lets you use your voice to control your computer in other ways.

This guide provides detailed information that will help you get the most out of using the program. It also explains how to ensure that Dragon NaturallySpeaking will recognize your speech accurately. Before using this guide, we recommend that you read the *Dragon NaturallySpeaking Quick Start* guide and view the online Tutorial.

This guide covers multiple editions of Dragon NaturallySpeaking. Where information applies to certain editions only, this is clearly noted.

Conventions used in this guide

1   This user's guide contains many examples of words and phrases you can say when using Dragon NaturallySpeaking. These examples usually appear in italics with quotation marks, for instance: *"Scratch That."*

2   Some procedures also include sample text for you to dictate. Sample text appears in a different typeface, with punctuation in square brackets. For example:

US/Canada: When talking to a computer [comma] try to say every word clearly without trailing off at the end of a sentence [period]

Other Dialects: When talking to a computer [comma] try to say every word clearly without trailing off at the end of a sentence [full stop]

3   This guide covers the five dialects of English that ship with Dragon NaturallySpeaking:

■   US English

- UK English
- Australian English
- Indian English
- Southeast Asian English

US English uses US spelling, punctuation, times, and currency. Dragon Systems recommends US English for Canadian users since this dialect formats numbers (including times, telephone numbers, and currency) in North American formats.

All other dialects use UK spelling, punctuation, times, and currency (some number settings depend on your Windows Regional Settings). Dictation examples that differ among dialects appear in a different font, as in this example:

- You can also correct a longer phrase by saying *"Correct [text] Through [text]"* (**US/Canada**) or *"Correct [text] To [text]"* (**Other Dialects**).

This user's guide uses US spelling and punctuation for consistency.

4 This guide also includes helpful tips to improve your dictation, and notes that require special attention. Tips and notes appear like this:

TIP *If you pause correctly, but Dragon NaturallySpeaking still types a command as dictation, you can force it to recognize what you say as a command by holding down the* CTRL *key.*

NOTE *The ability to create your own voice commands is available only in Dragon NaturallySpeaking Professional and higher editions.*

CHAPTER 1

Introducing Dragon NaturallySpeaking

Dragon NaturallySpeaking lets you talk to your computer instead of typing. As you talk, your words are transcribed onto your screen and into your documents or e-mail messages.

Talking to a computer while it types what you say is called *dictating*. You can dictate into Microsoft® Word, Corel® WordPerfect®, e-mail programs, personal information organizers, and virtually any other program in which you normally type.

You can use Dragon NaturallySpeaking for:

- Composing letters, memos, and e-mail messages. Just think about what you want to say, and then say it into the microphone.
- Writing a report, article, or story. Brainstorm out loud and capture your thoughts on screen. Then edit your work by voice or mouse and keyboard.
- "Typing up" notes from a meeting. When you get back to your desk, simply read your notes into the microphone.

You can also use simple voice commands to revise and format text, move around your document, and control your computer. Learn the basics in your *Quick Start* guide.

Dragon NaturallySpeaking isn't just for creating documents. You can also use your voice to start programs, open menus, and click buttons. If you use Internet Explorer, you can use Dragon NaturallySpeaking to browse the Web by voice. Learn how in Chapter 7, "Working With E-Mail and the Web."

If you share your computer with family members, friends, or colleagues, they can also use Dragon NaturallySpeaking. Simply create a new set of "user speech files" for each person who wants to talk to the computer. Find out how in Chapter 8, "Managing Users."

After you become comfortable talking to your computer, you may want to take the convenience of dictating a step further by using a portable recorder with Dragon NaturallySpeaking. This option is available if you have Dragon NaturallySpeaking Preferred or a higher edition. For more information, see Appendix A, "Using Dragon NaturallySpeaking With a Portable Recorder."

If you have Dragon NaturallySpeaking Professional or a higher edition, you can expand the power of using speech by creating your own voice commands. Find out how in Chapter 9, "Creating Your Own Dragon NaturallySpeaking Commands."

Dragon NaturallySpeaking Professional and higher editions also let you create and customize additional vocabularies for dictating in different subject areas. For more information, see "Managing vocabularies" on page 54.

What's new in version 5?

Dragon NaturallySpeaking version 5 has many new features to make your dictation easier and faster to use. Most of these features are available through the DragonBar. When you see the DragonBar on your screen, you can dictate into virtually any program.

Welcome to the DragonBar

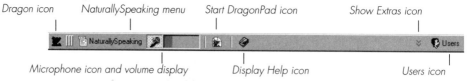

Dragon icon   NaturallySpeaking menu   Start DragonPad icon   Show Extras icon

Microphone icon and volume display   Display Help icon   Users icon

The Dragon icon
Click the icon (or right-click anywhere on the DragonBar) to display a menu that controls how the DragonBar looks and acts on your screen. See the online Help for more information.

NaturallySpeaking menu

The NaturallySpeaking menu on the DragonBar contains all the menu commands that you can use while working in Dragon NaturallySpeaking. Some of these commands are also available from other parts of the DragonBar, for example opening the online Help.

Microphone icon and volume display

Click the microphone icon to turn speech recognition on and off.

Microphone is off 🔇 Microphone is on and ready to dictate 🎤

The volume display shows how well the program is hearing your voice.

Start DragonPad icon

Click the icon to open the DragonPad, the built-in word processor for Dragon NaturallySpeaking.

Display Help icon

Click the icon to open online Help for Dragon NaturallySpeaking.

Users icon

Click the Users icon to display a menu that contains a list of your users and a command that opens the Manage Users dialog box.

Extras toolbar icon

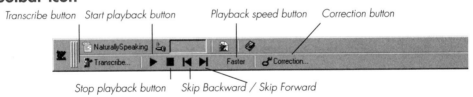

Transcribe button   Start playback button   Playback speed button   Correction button

Stop playback button   Skip Backward / Skip Forward

The Extras toolbar is available in Dragon NaturallySpeaking Preferred and higher editions.

Click the double chevron icon ⌄ to display the Extras toolbar, which contains the following:

Transcribe a recording button

Click this button to open the Transcribe dialog box, which you use to transcribe recordings of dictation made on portable recorders.

Playback toolbar

Contains controls that control the playback of your dictation. For more information, see "Playing back your dictation" on page 23, or see the online Help.

Playback speed button

Click this button to speed up or slow down dictation playback.

Correction button

Click this button to open the Correction dialog box and correct a mistake.

New features in Dragon NaturallySpeaking Standard and higher editions

Dictate into virtually any application

Whenever you see the DragonBar on your screen, you can dictate into any application and use many Dragon NaturallySpeaking commands. See "Which commands work in which programs?" on page 171 for more information.

Learn hands-on with a new online Tutorial

The Dragon NaturallySpeaking Tutorial leads you through basic dictation techniques. See your *Quick Start* guide and the online Help for more information.

Get started promptly

All computers that meet the minimum system requirements of the software now learn your voice in about 3 to 5 minutes. Your *Quick Start* guide takes you step-by-step from installation through your first dictation. See "Creating a new user" on page 132 of this user's guide for more information.

Dictate with improved accuracy

Dragon NaturallySpeaking version 5 continues to improve accuracy, from a company already recognized for its high recognition accuracy. See "Improving Your Speech Recognition" on page 31 for more information.

Choose quick and easy ways to correct mistakes

Proofread and correct your work as you dictate with the convenient Quick Correct list. See "Correcting recognition mistakes" on page 15 for more information.

Never forget a command again

Can't remember a command? Voice commands are readily available with helpful on-screen reminders, extensive online Help, a detachable command reference card, and two Top 10 Commands stickers for your keyboard and monitor. Say *"View Command List"* to see the Command List in the online Help, or see the "Dragon NaturallySpeaking Version 5 Commands List" on page 171 for a complete list of voice commands.

Add words from your documents quickly and easily

The new Add Words From Documents feature scans your documents for particular words you use and adds them to the Dragon NaturallySpeaking vocabulary in a few simple steps. See "Add Words from Documents" on page 35 for more information.

Manage your e-mail by voice

Dictate into popular e-mail programs with special built-in voice commands. See "Working with E-mail" on page 119 for more information.

Find new ways to surf the Web

New features and voice commands enhance your web browser. See "Working with Internet Explorer" on page 123 for more information.

New features in Dragon NaturallySpeaking Preferred and higher editions

Enter commonly used text

Create dictation shortcuts to insert multiple lines of text, such as a letter closing, with only a few words. See "Creating dictation shortcuts" on page 38 for more information.

Dictate in more than one language

Install multiple languages in the same edition of Dragon NaturallySpeaking (English-as-a-second-language editions only). See "Multilingual users" on page 137 for more information.

New features in Dragon NaturallySpeaking Professional and higher editions

Dictate now, correct later
Save a recording of your dictation session so that you or someone else can proofread and revise your work later. See "Dictate now, correct later" on page 26 for more information.

Work in Lotus® Notes®
Use new built-in commands, including Select-and-Say™ editing, in Lotus Notes. See the online Help for more information.

Organize and file your voice commands
Manage your macro scripts and specialized commands by placing them into multiple files. See "Creating and editing voice commands" on page 140 for more information.

Customize your own Tutorial
Dragon NaturallySpeaking resellers can customize the online Tutorial to include specific information about services that they provide.

All editions also feature many additional improvements and bug fixes.

What should I expect from Dragon NaturallySpeaking?

One reason to use Dragon NaturallySpeaking is to do your writing more quickly. Another is to reduce the stress associated with keyboarding. Or maybe you just like the idea of being able to lean back in your chair, put your feet up on the desk, and still get work done.

Dragon NaturallySpeaking is good for all these reasons, but making it work well requires some effort from you. Dragon NaturallySpeaking actually learns about your voice and pronunciation as you use it. When you use words the program doesn't know, it will make mistakes, and you'll have to stop and correct them.

It may take a while before you feel comfortable and productive using Dragon NaturallySpeaking. You can find out more about how to make the program work well by reading Chapter 2, "Using Dragon NaturallySpeaking Successfully."

Do I still need my mouse and keyboard?

Although you can use Dragon NaturallySpeaking to do almost everything on your computer by voice, some things are still easier to do by mouse or keyboard.

If using a mouse and keyboard is an option for you, try experimenting with using your voice and using your hands for different tasks, to see what works best. If using a mouse and keyboard is not an option, read Chapter 6, "Working With Your Desktop and Windows."

CHAPTER 2

Using Dragon NaturallySpeaking Successfully

If you followed the exercises in your *Quick Start* guide, by now you've had a chance to try dictating with Dragon NaturallySpeaking. So, are you ready to throw away your keyboard? Probably not. Chances are there are more mistakes in your document than you'd like to see.

Why does the program make mistakes, and what can be done so it makes them less often? This chapter provides some background information to help you understand how Dragon NaturallySpeaking works.

It then reveals the "Seven habits for success with Dragon NaturallySpeaking," a list of tips and procedures you can follow to make the program recognize your speech accurately. This discussion is continued in Chapter 3, "Improving Your Speech Recognition."

The section on "Correcting recognition mistakes" discusses how to correct misrecognized words, including ways to train the program to reduce future errors.

The chapter concludes by introducing dictation playback and text-to-speech (available in Dragon NaturallySpeaking Preferred and higher editions), and saving your dictation for later correction (available in Dragon NaturallySpeaking Professional and higher editions).

How Dragon NaturallySpeaking works

When you talk into the microphone, Dragon NaturallySpeaking doesn't hear words or phrases. The computer hears your speech as a continuous stream of sounds. From this stream, Dragon NaturallySpeaking picks out common sound patterns, known as *phonemes*.

To match these sound patterns to words, Dragon NaturallySpeaking relies on two large sources of data: *acoustic data* and *language data*.

Dragon NaturallySpeaking uses acoustic data about the sound patterns that make up different words to choose the words that most closely match what it heard. Since no two people sound exactly alike, Dragon NaturallySpeaking does a much better job of matching sounds to words when it knows something about your pronunciation. When you first trained the program, you provided acoustic data on top of what Dragon NaturallySpeaking already knows about the sounds of English.

Sometimes it's not possible for Dragon NaturallySpeaking to choose the correct word based on sound alone. Consider these two phrases: "pizza delivery boy" and "Pete's a delivery boy." When spoken, they sound almost exactly alike. How would Dragon NaturallySpeaking know which to choose?

Dragon NaturallySpeaking uses language data about the context and frequency of word use to determine which words were most likely spoken. The phrase "pizza delivery boy" is more common than "Pete's a delivery boy," so the program would favor this phrase over the other.

Since people write differently, it helps if Dragon NaturallySpeaking knows something about the frequency with which you use different words. When you Add Words From Documents, run Vocabulary Builder™, or make corrections to your dictation, you're providing the program with language data about how often you use different words.

Knowing that Dragon NaturallySpeaking uses acoustic data and language data to recognize your speech can help you know what to do to make the program work better.

Seven habits for success with Dragon NaturallySpeaking

The rest of this chapter, and Chapter 3, describe seven habits you can adopt to make Dragon NaturallySpeaking work well for you. If you make the techniques and procedures in these chapters a habit, and continue to use Dragon NaturallySpeaking regularly, you should be able to make the program recognize your speech more accurately.

Seven habits for success with Dragon NaturallySpeaking

Chapter 2

- Position your microphone correctly
- Speak properly to the computer
- Correct recognition mistakes

Chapter 3

- Add words to the Dragon NaturallySpeaking vocabulary
- Run Vocabulary Builder
- Train Dragon NaturallySpeaking to recognize problem words
- Run General Training again

If you have Dragon NaturallySpeaking Professional, you can also create specialized vocabularies to enhance recognition accuracy. See "Managing vocabularies" on page 54.

Positioning your microphone correctly

You've already heard a lot about the importance of your microphone position. If you followed the instructions on the screen when you first started Dragon NaturallySpeaking, your microphone is probably in about the right position. But you should continue to think about your microphone and check its position frequently to make sure it hasn't moved out of place.

If you find that Dragon NaturallySpeaking is making too many mistakes, experiment with moving the microphone a little closer to or farther from your mouth.

If extra words, such as "and" and "the," are often inserted into your document, Dragon NaturallySpeaking may be interpreting the sound of your breath as speech. Try moving the microphone slightly to the side, so it's not directly in front of your mouth.

Keep in mind that it's easy for the microphone to move slightly out of the best position. You might not notice if this happens, because Dragon NaturallySpeaking may still get most of your words right. But if the microphone is even slightly out of place, the program may no longer be able to tell the difference between similar-sounding words, such as "or" and "all," and will begin making subtle mistakes.

Make it a habit to check your microphone position regularly. If accuracy ever seems lower than normal, always start by checking your microphone.

TIP *You can double-check your microphone position at any time by running the Audio Setup Wizard. On the NaturallySpeaking menu, point to Advanced, then click Check Audio. Make sure your audio quality is "Passed."*

Speaking properly to the computer

At times the computer will type something that sounds like what you said but isn't quite right. People sometimes misunderstand each other in the same way. But the computer is not a person, so it won't help to:

SHOUT

t a l k s l o w l y

or. say. only. one. word. at. a. time.

This section provides some guidelines for talking to a computer.

Speak naturally and continuously, but pronounce each word clearly

When you talk to another person, you can mumble and run your words together and still be understood most of the time. For example, if you say, "Innit cold?" a person will probably understand that you're asking, "Isn't it cold?"

But Dragon NaturallySpeaking has trouble interpreting mumbled or slurred speech. The computer recognizes speech most accurately when it can hear each word distinctly.

To understand what it means to speak both clearly and naturally, listen to the way newscasters read the news. If you copy this style when you use Dragon NaturallySpeaking, you should see an improvement in how well the program recognizes what you say.

Make it a habit to say each word clearly when you talk to the computer.

Avoid leaving out words and making extra sounds (like "um")

In conversation with another person, it's okay if you leave out a word here and there. People are good at filling in the blanks in a sentence. Unfortunately, the computer is not very good at this. If you leave out words, Dragon NaturallySpeaking also leaves them out.

Another thing people do well is ignore all those "ums" and "ers" that show up in conversation. But the computer has no way of knowing which words are unimportant, so it simply transcribes everything you say.

Make it a habit to avoid leaving out words or making extra sounds. It may help to compose your thoughts before you speak.

Speak at your normal pace—don't slow down

When another person is having trouble understanding you, speaking more slowly usually helps. So it's not surprising that people often slow down and begin sounding out each syllable when Dragon NaturallySpeaking makes mistakes.

It doesn't help, however, to speak at an unnatural pace when you're talking to a computer. This is because the program listens for predictable sound patterns when matching sounds to words. If you speak in syllables, Dragon NaturallySpeaking is likely to transcribe each syllable as a separate word.

Make it a habit to speak at your normal pace, so Dragon NaturallySpeaking can learn your normal pronunciation.

Speak in phrases, rather than one word at a time

Along with the tendency to speak slowly, people often begin saying just one or two words at a time when Dragon NaturallySpeaking makes mistakes.

Surprisingly, speaking in very short phrases or individual words can actually lessen accuracy. This is because Dragon NaturallySpeaking uses the context of a phrase to help it decide what you said.

Consider the following phrase: "Dear Mr. Jones." If you were to dictate this phrase one word at a time (*"dear" "mister" "jones"*), Dragon NaturallySpeaking might type "Deer" or "Gear" instead of "Dear." But if you were to dictate the whole phrase (*"dear mister jones"*), the program can use context to determine that the word you want is most likely "Dear."

Make it a habit to dictate in phrases, so Dragon NaturallySpeaking can use context to help determine what you said. It may help to compose your thoughts before you speak.

Speak at your normal volume—don't whisper or speak too loudly

When you first started Dragon NaturallySpeaking and read the training text aloud, the program adapted to the pitch and volume of your voice, along with learning your pronunciation.

For this reason, you should continue to speak at a normal volume (or slightly louder if this helps). If you shout or whisper, Dragon NaturallySpeaking won't understand you as well.

Make it a habit to speak at your normal volume, since Dragon NaturallySpeaking has adjusted to this volume.

Prevent vocal strain

When you're dictating for long periods you should think about protecting your voice.

Here are some tips for preventing vocal strain:

- Sit up straight or stand in front of your computer.
- Don't speak in a loud voice or in any way that is stressful for you.
- Breathe deeply from your abdomen and not from the top of your chest.
- Loosen up and relax: stretch your arms, shoulders, neck, and jaw muscles.
- Take occasional breaks: get up, move around, and stretch.
- Keep your vocal cords moist: take sips of water and use a straw so you don't have to move the microphone out of place.

Correcting recognition mistakes

When Dragon NaturallySpeaking types the wrong words, you should correct these mistakes. By giving the program the right word, you actually teach the program not to make the same mistakes again.

Correcting mistakes requires some extra effort, but it saves you time in the long run by making Dragon NaturallySpeaking more accurate. You'll probably need to correct mistakes often when you first start dictating, and then less frequently as the program learns from your corrections.

Make it a habit to correct mistakes to continue to improve the accuracy of the program. Make sure you save your speech files when prompted, to preserve the adjustments the program makes.

Dragon NaturallySpeaking version 5 offers two tools for correcting:

- The Quick Correct list is the quickest and easiest way to make corrections in the DragonPad.
- The Correction dialog box is a more powerful tool that lets you correct text and spell new words.

Correcting mistakes with Quick Correct

In the DragonPad, correcting a mistake is quick and easy. Just select the mistake and choose the correct word or phrase from the Quick Correct list.

To correct a mistake with Quick Correct:

1 Dictate until Dragon NaturallySpeaking misrecognizes a word. For example, dictate this sentence:

US/Canada: The quick brown fox jumped over the lazy dog [period]

Other Dialects: The quick brown fox jumped over the lazy dog [full stop]

In the following example, Dragon NaturallySpeaking heard the word "quick" as "dark."

2 Select the mistake. You can select the text you just dictated by saying "*Select That,*" or you can select a specific word or phrase by saying "*Select*" followed by the word(s) you see. The Quick Correct list appears.

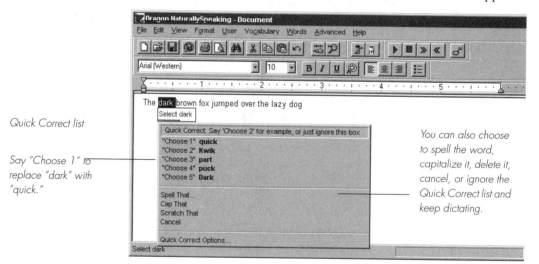

Quick Correct list

Say "Choose 1" to replace "dark" with "quick."

You can also choose to spell the word, capitalize it, delete it, cancel, or ignore the Quick Correct list and keep dictating.

In this example, when you say "select dark," the word "dark" is highlighted and the Quick Correct list shows you the most likely matches for the misrecognized word.

3 Choose the correct word from the Quick Correct list by saying *"Choose"* and the number next to your choice. In this example, say *"Choose 1,"* and "quick" will replace "dark."

If the word you want does not appear in the list, say *"Spell That"* or *"Correct That."* The Correction dialog box will appear for you to spell or type the correct word. See the next procedure for details.

When the Quick Correct list appears, you can also choose to:

- spell the word (in this example, say *"Spell That q-u-i-c-k"*)
- capitalize it (say *"Cap That,"* in this example, to get *"Dark"*)
- delete it (say *"Scratch That"*)
- say *"Cancel"* to dismiss the list
- ignore the Quick Correct list and keep dictating (in this example, just say *"quick"*)

If you ignore Quick Correct and dictate while text is selected, your new dictation will replace the selected text: this is called *Select-and-Say.* This method, however, does not teach Dragon NaturallySpeaking not to make the same mistake again. For more information on Select-and-Say, see "Select-and-Say vs. correction" on page 22.

TIP *If you prefer not to see the Quick Correct list every time you select text, you can turn it off. In the Options dialog box, select the Correction tab and clear the check box "Select commands bring up Quick Correct."*

The Quick Correct list works in the DragonPad, but not in other programs. If you select text by voice and the Quick Correct list does not appear, just say *"Spell That"* or *"Correct That"* and continue with the procedure below.

Using the Correction dialog box

The Correction dialog box is the most powerful and universal way to correct a mistake so that Dragon NaturallySpeaking won't misrecognize the word again.

There are many ways to open the Correction dialog box. Use the method that is most convenient for you, as described in the following list.

To open the Correction dialog box:

■ When the Quick Correct list is open, say *"Spell That"* or *"Correct That."* This method works only in the DragonPad.

■ To correct a mistake immediately after it appears, say *"Spell That"* or *"Correct That."* This method works in any program.

■ Say *"Correct"* and then the word or phrase that you see on the screen. This method works in Select-and-Say applications (see page 171).

■ You can also correct a longer phrase by saying *"Correct [text] Through [text]"* (**US/Canada**) or *"Correct [text] To [text]"* (**Other Dialects**). For [text], substitute the actual word or words at the beginning and the end of the phrase you want (they must be visible on the screen). For example, if you want to correct "it was a dark and stormy night," you can say *"Correct it was through night"* (**US/Canada**) or *"Correct it was to night"* (**Other Dialects**). This method works in Select-and-Say applications (see page 171).

■ Select text and say *"Spell That"* or *"Correct That."* This method works in Select-and-Say applications (see page 171).

■ Press the correction keyboard shortcut, the minus (-) key on the numeric keypad. This opens the Correction dialog box with the last thing you said, the selection, or the words preceding or following the insertion point.

■ Say *"Spell"* to open the Correction dialog box with no text in it. This allows you to spell a word for the first time. For more information, see "Spelling as you dictate" on page 22.

NOTE *If you're correcting more than one word, the words must all be in sequence (next to each other). You cannot use a single command to correct words that are in different parts of your document.*

Some people prefer to correct the mistakes in their documents by using the mouse and keyboard. You can use your mouse to select the wrong words (or simply place your insertion point somewhere in the mistake), and then press the minus (-) key on the numeric keypad to open the Correction dialog box.

To correct a word or phrase:

1 Open the Correction dialog box.

2 When the Correction dialog box opens, if the correct word or phrase is in the list of choices, you can simply choose it.

You can resize the Correction dialog box by dragging a corner or side.

Note: The Play Back button is only in Preferred and higher editions.

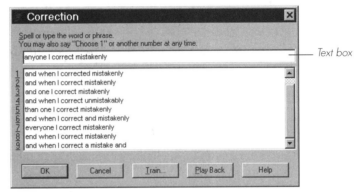

There are several ways to choose the correct text:

■ Say *"Choose"* and then the number of the correct choice. For example, say *"Choose 9"* (or *"Choose Numeral 9"*).

■ Click the correct choice, and then click or say *"OK."*

■ Double-click the correct choice.

This closes the Correction dialog box and enters the text into your document.

3 If none of the choices exactly matches what you said, you must enter the correct text. There are two ways to enter the correct text:

■ Start spelling the correct word or phrase. Say the letters continuously and quickly, not one at a time.

■ Start typing the correct word or phrase into the text box. As you type, the list shows alternatives that match what you've typed so far.

4 When you see the correct choice, choose it by voice or mouse.

5 If the correct choice doesn't appear, finish spelling or typing it and then click or say *"OK."* For example, try dictating the following text:

US/Canada: I liked your proposal period why don't you webify it and have the rest of the team take a look question mark

Other Dialects: I liked your proposal full stop why don't you webify it and have the rest of the team take a look question mark

Dragon NaturallySpeaking types:

I liked your proposal. Why don't you Web if I it and have the rest of the team take a look?

To correct the text, say "*Select Web if I,*" then "*Spell That w-e-b-i-f-y.*" Then click or say "*OK.*"

Spelling in the Correction dialog box

You can either spell text by voice or type it here. You cannot dictate whole words into the Correction dialog box.

When you're spelling, this is what you can say:

- letters (a–z)
- International Communications Alphabet (alpha, bravo, and so on)
- numbers (0–9)
- punctuation
- "Cap" (to capitalize the next letter)
- "Double" (to enter the next letter twice, for example, "*Double a*")
- "Space Bar" or "space" (to insert a space)
- "Backspace"
- "apostrophe ess"
- special characters (such as @, *, £, ©, and é)

For a complete list of special characters and the International Communications Alphabet, see "Correction dialog box commands" on page 177 of Appendix B.

When one of the choices in the Correction dialog box is almost correct, you can select it and use it as a starting point without entering the text into your document. Just click it or say "*Select*" (not "*Choose*") and then the number of the choice. For example, say "*Select 3*" (or "*Select Numeral 3*"). Then edit the word or phrase.

Editing in the Correction dialog box

When you're working in the Correction dialog box, you can use your voice to move the insertion point and to select and delete words and characters.

Moving around in the Correction dialog box

You can move the insertion point right or left by words or characters. For example, you can say *"Move Right a Word"* or *"Move Left 4 Characters."*

See the complete list below:

SAY	THEN *(one)*	THEN *(one)*
Move	Right	a Word *or* 1 Word
	Forward	2 Words
	Left	2..20 Words
	Back	a Character *or* 1 Character
		2 Characters
		2..20 Characters

Selecting text in the Correction dialog box

You can select all the text in the text box by saying *"Select Line"* or *"Select All."*

You can also select right or left by words or characters. For example, you can say *"Select Next Character"* or *"Select Previous 2 Words."* See the complete list below:

SAY	THEN *(one)*	THEN *(one)*
Select	Next	Word
	Forward	2 Words
	Previous	2..20 Words
	Back	Character
	Last	4 Characters
		2..20 Characters

Deleting text in the Correction dialog box

You can delete selected text in the Correction dialog box by saying *"Delete Selection."*

You can also delete words or characters. For example, you can say *"Delete Next Word"* or *"Delete Previous Character."*

See the complete list below:

SAY	THEN *(one)*	THEN *(one)*
Delete	Next	Word
	Forward	2 Words
	Previous	2..20 Words
	Back	Character
	Last	4 Characters
		2..20 Characters

Spelling as you dictate

With the new Spell command in Dragon NaturallySpeaking version 5, you can easily spell a word or phrase you want to dictate into your document. This can be useful if you are dictating a word that is not likely to be in the Dragon NaturallySpeaking vocabulary, such as a proprietary term or a foreign word.

To spell a word while dictating,

1 Spell the word. Say, for example, *"Spell c-i-a-o."*

You must say "Cap" if the word contains a capital letter. For example, say *"Spell Cap m-a-c Cap-m-i-l-l-a-n"* to type "MacMillan."

2 The Correction dialog box opens and Dragon NaturallySpeaking types the letters you spell. You can then continue spelling or correct any errors in the word you spelled.

For more tips on spelling, see the online Help.

Select-and-Say vs. correction

You can always make corrections by selecting your text and dictating to replace it. You learned about this method, called *Select-and-Say*, in the online Tutorial and the *Quick Start* guide. See "Which commands work in which programs?" on page 171 for a list of the programs that support Select-and-Say.

Selecting text and dictating over it, however, will not correct speech-recognition errors. Only by using the Quick Correct list or the Correction dialog box can you teach Dragon NaturallySpeaking not to make the same mistakes again.

For information on using Select-and-Say to revise your dictation, see "Using Select-and-Say" on page 90.

Playing back your dictation

Dictation playback is available in Dragon NaturallySpeaking Preferred and higher editions.

Playback commands work in the DragonPad, Microsoft Word 97 and 2000, Corel WordPerfect 8 and 9, and Lotus Notes.

Although Dragon NaturallySpeaking never makes a spelling mistake, the mistakes it does make can be challenging to find and fix. Sometimes, what the program types looks very different from what you actually said.

To make correcting mistakes easier, Dragon NaturallySpeaking records your voice as you dictate. You can play back your voice whenever you cannot tell by looking at your document what you originally said.

NOTE *Unless you have Dragon NaturallySpeaking Professional or a higher edition, playback is available only until you close a document. After you close a document, Dragon NaturallySpeaking deletes the recorded dictation for that document. See page 26 for information on saving dictation for later correction (Professional and higher editions).*

Playing back dictation in the Correction dialog box

When you're working in the Correction dialog box, click the Play Back button or say "*Play Back*" to play the dictation that goes with the words you're correcting. Then edit the text to match what you said.

You can set up Dragon NaturallySpeaking to play back dictation automatically whenever you open the Correction dialog box. On the NaturallySpeaking menu, point to Advanced, click Options, and then click the Correction tab. Select "Automatic playback on correction."

Sometimes, there's no dictation to play back. For example, you cannot play back text that wasn't entered by voice, such as words you typed or pasted into your document.

NOTE *Even when you have entered text by voice, you cannot play it back after you have cut it, copied it, pasted it, or otherwise moved it around in the document.*

If you have Dragon Naturally Speaking Professional or a higher edition, you can save your dictation with your document for later playback (see "Dictate now, correct later" on page 26). Otherwise, you cannot play back dictation after closing a document.

If dictation is not available, the Play Back button is dimmed (grayed out). When playback is not available, you may find text-to-speech useful for checking your work. See "Using text-to-speech" on page 28.

Playing back dictation in a document

To help you check your work for mistakes, you can play back a line, a paragraph, a selection, or the whole document. After playback starts, you can stop it as soon as you notice a mistake and automatically open the Correction dialog box.

The Playback toolbar is an extra section of the DragonBar that is normally hidden. To see the Playback toolbar, click the double chevron icon ⌄ on the DragonBar to open the Extras toolbar (Preferred and higher editions).

To play back dictation:

To play back dictation, do any of the following:

■ Select the text you want to play back, and say *"Play That Back."*

■ Click the Start Playback button on the Playback toolbar.

Start Playback

■ Move the insertion point to the text you want to play back and say any of the following commands:

SAY	TO
Play Back Line	Play back dictation for the current line.
Play Back Paragraph	Play back dictation for the current paragraph.
Play Back Document	Play back dictation for the whole document.
Play Back Window	Play back dictation for the text in view.
Play Back to Here	Play back dictation from the top of the document window to the insertion point.
Play Back from Here	Play back dictation from the insertion point to the bottom of the document window.

To stop playback:

To stop playback, do any of the following:

■ Click the Stop Playback button on the Playback toolbar.

Stop Playback

■ Click anywhere in the document window.

■ Press the ESC key.

(It's not possible to stop playback by voice, because the computer cannot hear speech input when it's playing back dictation.)

To skip backward or forward:

You can skip backward or forward in your document by a few words. To skip backward or forward, do one of the following:

■ To skip backward a few words, click the Skip Backward button on the Playback toolbar.

Skip Backward   Skip Forward

■ To skip forward a few words, click the Skip Forward button on the Playback toolbar.

To stop playback and correct a mistake:

To stop playback and correct a mistake, do any of the following:

- Click the Correction button on the Playback toolbar.

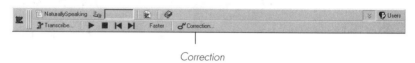

Correction

- Press the minus (-) key on the numeric keypad.

This stops playback and simultaneously opens the Correction dialog box. There you can correct the text for the last phrase played back.

> **NOTE** By default, Dragon NaturallySpeaking stores about 30 minutes of dictation (40 MB). If you want to be able to store more dictation, you can change the amount of disk space that's set aside for storing it. On the NaturallySpeaking menu, point to Advanced, click Options, and then click the Miscellaneous tab. Increase the number in the "Disk space reserved for speech data" box.

Dictate now, correct later

When you dictate into the DragonPad, you can save your dictation with your text so either you or someone else can correct it later. You must create and edit your file in the DragonPad to be able to play back dictation. This feature is available in Dragon NaturallySpeaking Professional and higher editions.

You can save dictation with your document if you select the Prompt to Save Dictation with Document box on the Startup/Shutdown tab of the Options dialog. The first time you save a document in DragonPad during an editing session, Dragon NaturallySpeaking asks you whether you want to save your speech data. If you save your speech data, you can reopen the document at a later time and play back your dictation. If you do not save your speech data, your dictation is stored only during the current editing session.

Correcting your own dictation

If you save your dictation, you can open your file later and play back and correct the text as if you had just dictated it.

Correcting someone else's dictation

You can play back someone else's dictation and correct the text to match the dictation. You can do this in two ways:

■ You can correct the dictation using your user files.

■ You can correct the dictation using the document author's user files.

Correcting with your user files

You should use this correction technique if you regularly correct another person's text by voice and it is not important to maximize the author's recognition accuracy.

When you use your user files, you can correct the dictation just as you would correct your own dictation, using any combination of voice commands and keyboard typing. Even though you are correcting someone else's dictation, your work won't reduce recognition accuracy for either you or the person who dictated the text. But your corrections to the other person's dictation won't improve recognition either.

Correcting with the document author's user files

You should use this correction technique if you do not need to correct by voice and it is important to maximize the author's recognition accuracy.

TIP *This technique works if all work is done on a single computer. Consult your Dragon NaturallySpeaking reseller about ways to dictate on one computer and correct on another.*

If you correct dictation using the author's user files, you must not correct by voice, or you may reduce that person's recognition accuracy. You can, however, improve the author's recognition accuracy if you make corrections by using the keyboard and mouse with the Quick Correct list or Correction dialog box. See the following procedure for details.

To correct using someone else's user files:

1 Make sure you are not wearing the microphone headset, or that the microphone is not turned on or plugged in. This will ensure that you don't accidentally reduce the accuracy of someone else's user files by using your voice.

2 Make sure the DragonPad Extras toolbar is displayed so you can see the playback command buttons.

3 Open the user files of the person whose text you will correct.

4   In DragonPad, open the document to correct.

5   Use the buttons on the Extras toolbar to play back dictation.

6   Select the text you want to correct by mouse or keyboard.

7   Press the correction hot key (normally the minus [-] key on the numeric key pad) or click the Correct button on the DragonBar Extras toolbar. The Quick Correct list or Correction dialog box appears with the selected text.

8   Use the keyboard to correct the text.

9   Save the text and the user's speech files when you are done.

Using text-to-speech

Text-to-speech is available in Dragon NaturallySpeaking Preferred and higher editions.

You can use text-to-speech to have text on your screen (not your current dictation) read aloud in a computer voice. For example, you can have a document that you (or someone else) dictated read back while you listen for mistakes and sections you may want to revise.

Text-to-speech is available only in the DragonPad, Microsoft Word, and Corel WordPerfect. You can, however, copy and paste text from other programs and then use text-to-speech.

To start text-to-speech:

To start text-to-speech, do any of the following:

- Select the text you want to hear (a line, a paragraph, and so on), and then say *"Read That."*

- Select the text you want to hear, and then select Read That from the Advanced submenu (or right-click in your document and click Read That from the shortcut menu).

■ Move the insertion point to the text you want to hear and say any of the following commands:

SAY	TO
Read Line	Read back the current line.
Read Paragraph	Read back the current paragraph.
Read Document	Read back the whole document.
Read Window	Read back the text in view.
Read to Here	Read back from the top of the document window to the insertion point.
Read from Here	Read back from the insertion point to the bottom of the document window.

To stop text-to-speech:

To stop text-to-speech, do any of the following:

■ From the NaturallySpeaking menu, point to Advanced and click Stop Playback/Reading.

■ Right-click in your document and click Stop Playback/Reading from the shortcut menu.

■ Press the ESC key.

You can control the speed, pitch, volume, and other text-to-speech settings. From the NaturallySpeaking menu, point to Advanced, click Options, and then click the Text-to-speech tab.

Notes on correcting with another author's user files

This technique works if all work is done on a single computer. Consult your Dragon NaturallySpeaking reseller about ways to dictate on one computer and correct on another.

To display the DragonBar Extras toolbar, click the double chevron icon ⌄ on the DragonBar. You cannot display the Extras toolbar if the DragonBar is in cling mode.

In the Quick Correct list, you can use the mouse or keyboard to select any of the commands displayed below the correction choices. For example, you can click *"Spell That"* to open the Correction dialog box and spell the word.

You may want to select the following on the Correction tab of the Options dialog box:

■ "Correct" command brings up Correction dialog box
■ Automatic playback on correction box

With these settings, Dragon NaturallySpeaking will automatically play back the author's dictation for each text selection you correct. The Quick Correct list does not play back dictation.

When you correct someone else's dictation, make sure that the amount of disk space you have reserved for storing dictation is at least as large as the amount allocated for the user that created the text. You alllocate the disk space on the Miscellaneous tab of the Options dialog box.

Saving dictation with documents can take up a lot of disk space, typically more than a megabyte per minute of dictation. To save this space, delete any dictation you no longer need. Dragon NaturallySpeaking saves dictation in a file with the same name as the document, but with the extension .dra. For example, if you dictate a document called MyDoc.rtf and save your dictation, Dragon NaturallySpeaking saves your dictation in a file called MyDoc.dra in the same directory as your document.

Improving Your Speech Recognition

Working with the Dragon NaturallySpeaking vocabulary

If Dragon NaturallySpeaking gets a word wrong, it could be that the word is not in the program's *vocabulary*. When this is the case, you need to teach Dragon NaturallySpeaking the new word so that it can recognize it when you say it.

This chapter talks about the vocabulary used by Dragon NaturallySpeaking, which contains both active words and backup words. Version 5 has quick and easy ways to add new words to your vocabulary. As well as adding words when correcting mistakes, you can now:

- add an individual word
- add words from documents
- create dictation shortcuts for frequently used text (Preferred and higher editions)

Dragon NaturallySpeaking also offers more powerful tools for more advanced vocabulary building. Vocabulary Builder™ (see page 44) and Vocabulary Editor™ (see page 41) give you more control for customizing your vocabulary. In Dragon NaturallySpeaking Professional and higher editions, you can create, import, and export multiple vocabularies. See the section on "Managing vocabularies" on page 54 for details.

The next section discusses how to train Dragon NaturallySpeaking to recognize problem words, including voice commands. Finally, the chapter concludes by explaining when and how to run General Training again to improve your recognition accuracy.

About the vocabulary

The Dragon NaturallySpeaking vocabulary contains the words the program can recognize when you say them. The vocabulary contains thousands of words and their common pronunciations. It also contains language data about how frequently words are used alone and in combination with others.

When you first start Dragon NaturallySpeaking, it creates a standard vocabulary on your computer. A vocabulary contains *active words* (the *active vocabulary*) and *backup words* (the *backup dictionary*).

Active words

The most commonly used vocabulary words are kept *active* (stored in computer memory). When you dictate these words, Dragon NaturallySpeaking is likely to get them right on the first try (that is, without requiring you to do anything extra, such as correcting the words).

For example, all the words in the following sentence are active (including "Mbeki"), so Dragon NaturallySpeaking should be able to recognize them all correctly on the first try.

Today [comma] the Prime Minister met President Mbeki of South Africa

Don't worry that the words you want to say won't be active. The list of active words is very long and continually changes (as you correct mistakes) to always include words you're likely to use.

Backup dictionary words

All the vocabulary words that are not currently active are kept in the backup dictionary (stored on your computer's hard disk, not in memory). Dragon NaturallySpeaking can recognize words in the backup dictionary, but not on the first try.

If Dragon NaturallySpeaking has trouble recognizing a word, it may mean that this word is only in the backup dictionary. You can add a word to the active vocabulary by correcting it (see "Correcting recognition mistakes" on page 15).

To add a word by correcting it:

1 Dictate the following sentence. The word "Punxsutawney" (pronounced punks-ah-tawny) is in the backup dictionary, not the active vocabulary, so Dragon NaturallySpeaking won't recognize it correctly on the first try.

Meet me in Punxsutawney [comma] Pennsylvania

When the program makes a mistake (for example, types "punk said Tony" instead of "Punxsutawney"), correct the mistake.

2 (In the DragonPad) Select the mistake by saying *"Select punk said Tony."* The Quick Correct list will appear with the most likely choices for the word you selected.

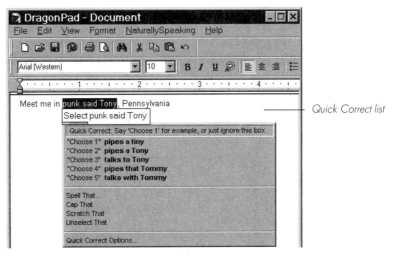

Quick Correct list

NOTE *"Select" commands and the Quick Correct list are available in the DragonPad (see page 16), but steps 1–3 may not work in all programs. To correct a word and make it active in any program, you can always select the word by voice or mouse and then say "Spell That" (steps 4 and 5).*

3 If the word you want appears in the Quick Correct list, say (for example) *"Choose 2."* You can say any number that appears in the list.

If the word you want does not appear in the Quick Correct list, or if the Quick Correct list does not appear at all, select the word by voice or mouse and use steps 4 and 5 below.

4 Say *"Spell That"* or *"Correct That."* The Correction dialog box opens.

5 Type or spell the correction in the Correction dialog box.

Since "Punxsutawney" is in the backup dictionary, it should appear in the list of alternatives before you finish entering it. (The list of alternatives always displays possible endings for the text in the text box.)

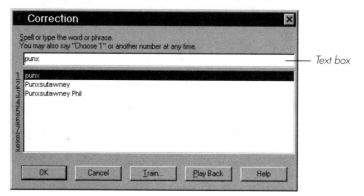

6 Say, for example, ""*Choose 2.*" You can also select the correct word and click or say *"OK."*

The Correction dialog box closes and "Punxsutawney" becomes an active word. The next time you dictate "Punxsutawney," Dragon NaturallySpeaking should get it right.

7 Save your speech files to add the word to your active vocabulary.

Quick and easy ways to add new words

When Dragon NaturallySpeaking gets a word wrong, often it's because the word is not in the vocabulary at all. This is likely if the word is an uncommon name or specialized term. You must teach Dragon NaturallySpeaking these new words, so it can recognize them when you say them.

Version 5 has quick and easy ways to add new words to your vocabulary. You can:

- Add words when correcting mistakes (see previous procedure)
- Add and train individual words
- Add words from documents

This next section describe how to add and train an individual word, and how to add words from documents. This section also tells you how to create dictation shortcuts for commonly used words and phrases (see page 38).

The section on "Advanced tools for building and editing vocabularies" on page 41 discusses more powerful ways to work with vocabularies.

Make it a habit to teach Dragon NaturallySpeaking new words to continue to improve the accuracy of the program. Make sure you save your speech files, when prompted, to preserve these changes to your vocabulary.

Adding an individual word

To add and train an individual word:

1 From the NaturallySpeaking menu, point to Words and click Add Individual Word. Spell or type the word you want to add to the vocabulary. If you want to train the pronunciation of the word (usually a good idea), leave the check box selected. Then click or say "*Add.*"

2 The Train Words dialog box will open with the word you have added. Click or say "*Record*" to begin recording, then say the word as you normally pronounce it. Click or say "*Done*" to close the dialog box and add the word to your vocabulary.

Add Words from Documents

Add Words from Documents is a quick and easy way to add any new words in a document or folder to the vocabulary. For example, if you have an online address book or a list of employee names, you can use Add Words from Documents to quickly identify all the words that are not in the vocabulary and add them.

This procedure will add:

- Words that match backup dictionary words with the same capitalization, for example, Punxsutawney or jackstraws

- Unexpected capitalizations of words found in the active or backup dictionaries, for example, "I'll see you at the Meeting today"

- Words with at least one uppercase letter that are not in the backup dictionary, for example, eBusiness and Brooklynese, or a name, such as Rusinow

NOTE *The program expects to find capitals at the beginning of sentences, or in a sequence of words that are all capitalized or have initial caps, such as a book title. It does not expect to find capitals in the middle of words or sentences.*

This procedure will *not* add all-lowercase words that are not in the backup dictionary.

You have more choices over which words are added when you run Vocabulary Builder (see page 48), but Add Words from Documents is quicker and designed more specifically to process proper names, such as a company e-mail list.

TIP *Before running Add Words from Documents, you may want to prepare your documents as described on page 45 to make sure that they are in readable format and free of spelling errors.*

To Add Words from Documents:

1 From the NaturallySpeaking menu, point to Words and click Add Words from Documents. The Add Words from Documents dialog box opens.

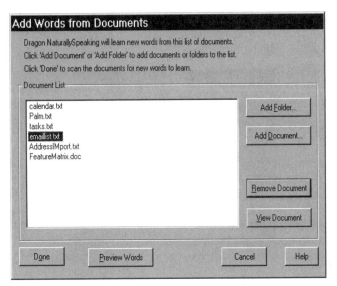

▲ *The Add Words from Documents dialog box lets you add all the documents in a folder or add documents one at a time. Select any document in the list to remove or view it.*

2 Click or say *"Add Document."* Navigate to the documents you want to add and select them.

3 (optional) Click or say *"Add Folder."* This will add all the documents in the folder you select.

   TIP *You can often achieve very good results by skipping directly to Step 6.*

4 (optional) To view any document in the list, select it and click or say *"View Document."*

5 (optional) Click or say *"Preview Words"* to see a checklist of words (from all the documents in the list) that are not in your current vocabulary.

   ■ Add only words you think you'll use frequently, not ones you're unlikely to need.

■ Don't add capitalized words unless you plan to dictate the capitalized form of the word often (for example, a pet's name "Fluffy").

To remove a word from the list of words to be added to your active vocabulary, clear the check box for that word in the Preview Words dialog box.

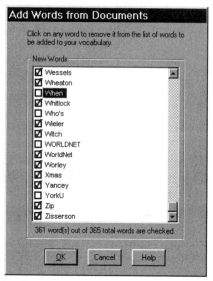

▲ *The Preview Words dialog box in Add Words From Documents lets you select or remove words from the list to be added. Clear any check box to remove a word from the list.*

6 Click "Done" to scan the documents for the words you want to add to the vocabulary. Your speech files will be updated and saved automatically.

Creating dictation shortcuts

A *dictation shortcut* is a quick way to insert frequently used text into your document. You can create dictation shortcuts for text that you use often or text that is complicated to dictate. In Dragon NaturallySpeaking version 5 (Preferred and higher editions), you can even create dictation shortcuts for multiple lines of text.

For example, you could create a shortcut that types your name and address whenever you say *"My Signature."* In the example below, the written form for the dictation shortcut appears on the left, and the spoken form is "*My Signature.*"

WRITTEN FORM	SPOKEN FORM
Michael D. Bowman 25 Main Street Wilmington, DE 12345	my signature
This message was dictated with Dragon NaturallySpeaking Professional on a Dragon NaturallyMobile recorder.	my mobile signature

To create a dictation shortcut:

1 From the NaturallySpeaking menu, point to Words and click Dictation Shortcuts.

2 In the Spoken form box, type the phrase you want to say to insert the written form text.

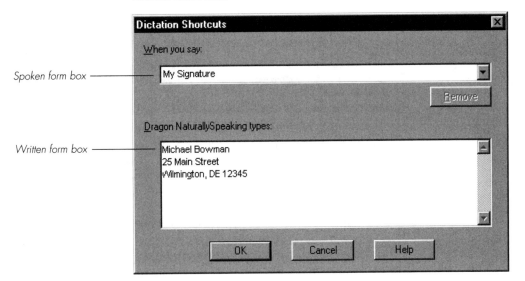

Spoken form box

Written form box

3 In the Written form box, type the text you want typed into your document. Text can be up to 1,000 characters and may include line and paragraph breaks.

Here are some guidelines for selecting a spoken form:

- Try to use unique phrases—don't use a phrase you might want to use in your writing.

- Don't use a single word as the spoken form.

- Make the spoken form something easy to remember.

- Use real words; otherwise, Dragon NaturallySpeaking may not know how they are pronounced and will prompt you to train them.

- If you use letters, put a space between them and a period (**US/ Canada**) or full stop (**Other Dialects**) after each one (for example, J. V. O.).

- (optional) For consistency with other Dragon NaturallySpeaking commands, capitalize each word in the dictation shortcut name.

4 Click or say "*OK.*"

Dragon NaturallySpeaking adds the dictation shortcut to the vocabulary. When you dictate the spoken form, the program now enters the written form into your document. For more information on spoken vs. written forms, see "More about spoken forms" on page 43.

TIP *Dictation shortcuts are commands, so you must pause before and after saying them. If you have a word or short phrase that fits on one line, and you want to be able to dictate it differently from the way it's spelled, you should enter a spoken form for the word in Vocabulary Editor rather than creating a dictation shortcut. See "To create a spoken form for a word:" on page 43.*

With Dragon NaturallySpeaking Professional and higher editions, you can also create your own voice commands for inserting frequently used text and controlling your computer by voice. See Chapter 9, "Creating Your Own Dragon NaturallySpeaking Commands" on page 139.

You may want to train Dragon NaturallySpeaking to recognize words you add to your vocabulary by pronouncing them correctly. See "Training Dragon NaturallySpeaking to recognize problem words" on page 59 for information on the many ways to train words.

Advanced tools for building and editing vocabularies

The NaturallySpeaking Words submenu offers quick and easy ways to add and train words. For more powerful tools to work with your vocabulary, you can turn to the features of the NaturallySpeaking Advanced submenu. You can use Advanced vocabulary tools to:

- edit your vocabulary with Vocabulary Editor
- build your vocabulary with Vocabulary Builder
- manage vocabularies (if you have more than one, for Dragon NaturallySpeaking Professional and higher editions)

The following sections describe each Advanced tool and how to use it.

Editing your vocabulary

The Vocabulary Editor shows you all the *active* words (the most commonly used words) in the Dragon NaturallySpeaking vocabulary. You can open Vocabulary Editor to find out whether a word is in the active vocabulary. If it's not there, you can add it. If it is, you can create a different spoken form.

TIP *Want to check to see if a word is already in the vocabulary? Type the first few letters of the word into the Written form box. If the word is in the vocabulary, it will appear on the screen.*

To edit your vocabulary:

1 On the NaturallySpeaking menu, point to Advanced, then click Edit Vocabulary.

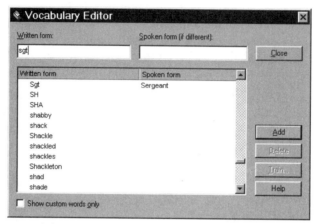

▲ *Vocabulary Editor lists all the active words in the Dragon NaturallySpeaking vocabulary.*

A word's written form is what Dragon NaturallySpeaking types when you say the word. The spoken form is how you say the word. For example, the spoken form for "Sgt." is *"Sergeant."*

Words you have added are marked with a colored star ✳ (not including any words that were previously in the backup dictionary). To see only the words you have added, click "Show custom words only."

2 Type the new word or phrase into the Written form box. Leave the Spoken form box empty, unless the word or phrase is not pronounced the way it's spelled (as in the example pictured). If so, see "To create a spoken form for a word:" on page 43.

> **NOTE** *You can use the Dictation Shortcuts tool for phrases longer than 128 characters—even multiple lines—that you use frequently. You can learn about dictation shortcuts on page 38.*

3 Click Add.

Some special words (for example, "New Paragraph") have a blank written form. These words are built into Dragon NaturallySpeaking. You cannot add your own words with a blank written form.

More about spoken forms

Perhaps your vocabulary contains proprietary words with unusual capitalization, or proper names with unusual spellings. Some phrases, such as company names, have particular punctuation. Or, you might want Dragon NaturallySpeaking to write out a person's name when you say their initials. You can teach the program to type the word or phrase correctly when it recognizes the spoken form.

TIP *You can also create a spoken form for a word you're having trouble getting Dragon NaturallySpeaking to recognize (for example, if the program often types "Lara" when you say "Laura" and correcting and training the word doesn't help). In the last example in the table, the written form for the word would be "Laura" and the spoken form should be a unique phrase, such as "Laura my office mate."*

For any word or short phrase that is less than 128 characters and fits on a single line, you should create a spoken form rather than a dictation shortcut (see page 38).

Here are some examples of words with different written and spoken forms. Look in the Vocabulary Editor window for more examples.

WRITTEN FORM	SPOKEN FORM
eBusiness	ee business
Daniell	Daniel with two ells
Niamh	Nev
CINCPAC	sink pack
mdbowman@company.com	my e-mail address
Robert F. Kennedy	R. F. K.
Waldron, Lichtin & Foust	Waldron Lichtin and Foust
(617) 965-5200	my phone number

To create a spoken form for a word:

1 On the NaturallySpeaking menu, point to Advanced, then click Edit Vocabulary.

2 Find the word you want in the list by typing the first few letters in the Written form box.

NOTE *If the word you want to edit doesn't appear in Vocabulary Editor, it means the word isn't in the active vocabulary. You need to add it to the active vocabulary before you can edit it. (See "Editing your vocabulary" on page 41.)*

3 Select the word.

4 Type the new spoken form into the Spoken Form box. Make sure you type it exactly as is it pronounced.

5 (optional) Make any changes, such as punctuation or capitalization, to the Written Form box.

6 Click Add. This adds the word with your changes.

7 If the word was already in the active vocabulary before you edited it, you should then delete the original word.

To delete a word from the vocabulary:

Normally, you don't need to delete words from the vocabulary. But if a word is regularly confused with another one that you never use, you might want to delete the one you don't use.

To delete a word, select it and click Delete. (You can select multiple words by holding down the CTRL key while you click. Clicking while holding the SHIFT key will select consecutive words.)

Some common words (like "the") cannot be deleted, since Dragon NaturallySpeaking wouldn't understand you very well without them.

Building your vocabulary

Running Vocabulary Builder teaches Dragon NaturallySpeaking about your vocabulary and writing style. If Dragon NaturallySpeaking knows what words you use in your writing and how you put them together, it can do a better job of recognizing what you say when you dictate.

Like Add Words from Documents, Vocabulary Builder works by "reading" documents you've already written on the computer. It uses these documents to gather language data about the frequency of words you use and the order in which they typically appear. For example, if Vocabulary Builder were analyzing this guide, it would learn that the word "Dragon" is used frequently and the words "by voice" often appear together. Dragon NaturallySpeaking would then know to favor these words over similar-sounding words.

Vocabulary Builder also gives you more control than Add Words from Documents over how words are added to your vocabulary. By building your vocabulary, you can:

- add words from a predefined list
- add words that are not in the backup dictionary
- filter and sort words before you add them
- choose whether to adapt to your document style
- view a statistical summary of your Vocabulary Builder session

You may want to run Vocabulary Builder if Dragon NaturallySpeaking is still making many mistakes, or any time you have documents you'd like to analyze. You can run Vocabulary Builder as often as you like without overwriting language data gathered previously.

To run Vocabulary Builder, you need to complete the following steps:

- Prepare documents (see page 45)
- Add words from a list (optional; see page 46)
- Run Vocabulary Builder
- Add words found in documents

The following section describes each step.

Preparing documents

Start by finding documents on your computer that are good examples of the kind of text you'll be dictating when you use Dragon NaturallySpeaking.

For example, if you plan to dictate memos and e-mail messages, find some correspondence you've already written. Your e-mail outbox is a good source of text. Any documents you're working on currently are also good ones to use. The more documents you can use, the better.

NOTE *It's okay to process documents you didn't write, but only if they are similar in style to your own writing (for example, a report written by a colleague in the same profession).*

To prepare documents:

1 Make sure documents are in the following formats:

- .TXT (Text)
- .RTF (Rich Text Format)
- .DOC (Microsoft Word version 6.0 or later)
- .WPD (Corel WordPerfect version 8 or 9)
- .HTM or .HTML (Hypertext Markup Language)
- .SHTM or .SHTML (Server-side include Hypertext Markup Language)

TIP *Dragon NaturallySpeaking can process.TXT (text) files faster than other formats. Consider using text files whenever possible.*

Dragon NaturallySpeaking can process Microsoft Word and Corel WordPerfect files only if you have the corresponding word processor installed on your computer. If it's not installed, convert the documents to another format, such as .TXT.

If you want to process your e-mail messages (a good idea if you'll be using Dragon NaturallySpeaking to write e-mail), you'll need to either export the text into one of the formats listed above, or copy and paste messages into a new document.

NOTE *E-mail headers may contain characters that Dragon NaturallySpeaking cannot process. If the program cannot process your e-mail text, try deleting all the header information from the file.*

2 Use a spelling checker to correct any spelling mistakes in the documents. This will prevent misspelled words from being identified as new words to be added to the vocabulary.

Once you've prepared your documents, you're ready to add them to your vocabulary.

Adding words from a list

If you're new to Dragon NaturallySpeaking, you can skip this step or do it later. After you become familiar with adding words to your vocabulary, you may find adding words from a list to be a helpful feature.

When Dragon NaturallySpeaking analyzes your documents, it starts by displaying a list of all the new words found, so you can select the ones you want to add to the vocabulary. If the list is very long, selecting and editing words can be time-consuming. Therefore, Dragon NaturallySpeaking also gives you the option of adding a list of words directly to the vocabulary. You can add this list as a document in Add Words from Documents (see page 35), or by selecting "Add words from a list" in Vocabulary Builder before processing documents.

Adding words from a list saves you time and also offers other advantages. You can include frequently used phrases in your list to improve recognition of these phrases. For example, if Dragon NaturallySpeaking has trouble recognizing the name "Ellen Cohen" even though both "Ellen" and "Cohen" are in the vocabulary, you can add the phrase "Ellen Cohen" to the vocabulary.

To create a list of words:

Create a text (.TXT) file and enter each word or phrase you want to add to the vocabulary on a separate line. Make sure words are spelled correctly.

TIP *To include a spoken form, type a backslash (\) and then the spoken form. The spoken form will appear in the Spoken form box in Vocabulary Editor after the word is added. See page 42 for an illustration of written and spoken forms.*

Following is an example of a correctly formatted list:

Each line is added to the vocabulary as a single item. In this example, the phrases "Ellen Cohen," "Fluffy the Cat," and so on, will be added.

▲ *You can use the DragonPad to create your text file.*

Running Vocabulary Builder

Prepare your documents and create a list of words to add (optional), following the procedures described in the previous step. Once you have one or more documents prepared, you're ready to run Vocabulary Builder.

To run Vocabulary Builder:

1 Open the user and vocabulary you want to personalize.

> **NOTE** *In Dragon NaturallySpeaking Professional or higher editions, each user may have more than one vocabulary. From the NaturallySpeaking menu, point to Advanced and click Manage Vocabularies. Then select the vocabulary you want to personalize and click Open.*

2 From the Dragon NaturallySpeaking menu, point to Advanced and click Build Vocabulary. The Vocabulary Builder Wizard appears.

3 Follow the instructions on the screen.

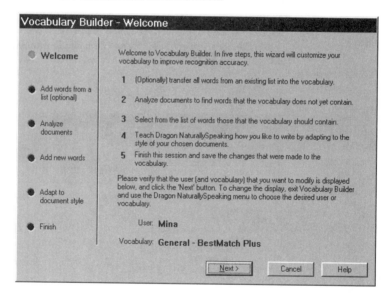

To add words from a list (optional):

1 In the Add Words from a List dialog box, specify a file containing words you want to add to the vocabulary. (See "Adding words from a list" on page 46 for more information about this step.)

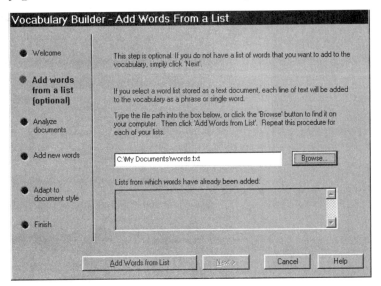

2 If you specify a file, click Add Words from List and then click Next to continue.

TIP *You can add word lists from multiple files. The wizard tells you how.*

To skip this step, just click Next.

To analyze documents:

1 In the Analyze Documents dialog box, click Add.

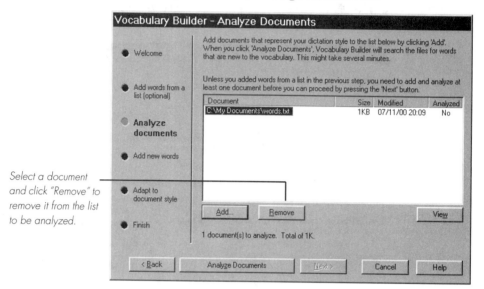

Select a document and click "Remove" to remove it from the list to be analyzed.

▲ *Vocabulary Builder uses documents you've written to teach Dragon NaturallySpeaking how you write.*

2 In the Analyze Documents dialog box, find and select the documents you want to process,* and then click Open.

> **NOTE** *You can select multiple documents in one folder by holding down the CTRL key while you click. To select a range of documents, hold down the SHIFT key while you click. To add documents from a different folder, click Add again.*

Documents you select are added to the Analyze Documents dialog box. If you need to remove a document, select it and click Remove.

3 To start processing the documents, click Analyze Documents.

> **NOTE** *If Vocabulary Builder displays an error message, it may mean that one or more of your files is not in the correct format (see the list of acceptable formats on page 46) or that the program used to create one of your files is not installed on your computer.*

---

* *Although there's no limit on the size or number of documents you can analyze, Vocabulary Builder analyzes only the first 500,000 words each time you run it.*

After a document is processed, the word "Yes" appears in the Analyzed column.

4 When you're finished processing documents, click Next.

After Vocabulary Builder analyzes documents, it displays the Add New Words dialog box with a list of the new words found.

Click ☑ *to select words to add to the vocabulary*

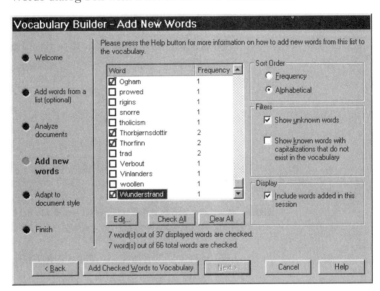

If there are words on the list that you use frequently, you can add them to the vocabulary to improve accuracy, but this step is not required. The Add New Words dialog box displays all the words found that are not in the Dragon NaturallySpeaking vocabulary (neither the active vocabulary nor the backup dictionary).

To add new words found in documents (optional):

1 Use the Filter and Display options if you want to show or hide words in the list.

- Select "Show unknown words" to view words found that are not in the vocabulary in any form (for example, "Anelka"). This option filters out words such as "Fluffy," where the lowercase form of the word ("fluffy") is already in the vocabulary.

- Select "Show known words with capitalizations that do not exist in the vocabulary" to view words that are in the vocabulary but were found with unusual capitalization (for example, "Fluffy" and "joan").

NOTE *Any capitalized words found at the beginning of a sentence or in a title (such as "War and Peace") don't appear in the list.*

■ Clear the "Include words added in this session" box if you want to hide any words that you have added since you began running Vocabulary Builder this time.

2 Click to select the words you want to add to the vocabulary.

■ Add only words you think you'll use frequently, not ones you're unlikely to need.

■ Don't add capitalized words unless you plan to dictate the capitalized form of the word often (for example, a pet's name "Fluffy").

3 If a word you want to add contains a spelling or capitalization error, select the word and click Edit (or double-click the word).

TIP *There's no need to edit a misspelled word and add it to the vocabulary if it's already in the vocabulary with correct spelling.*

In the Edit Word dialog box, correct the written form of the word. Leave the Spoken form box empty unless the word is not pronounced the way it's spelled. To remove capital letters automatically, click Lowercase.

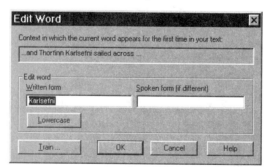

▲ *Use the Edit Word dialog box to correct spelling and capitalization errors before adding words to the vocabulary.*

When you have finished editing, click OK to return to the Add New Words dialog box.

4   After selecting and editing words you want to add, click Add Checked Words to Vocabulary.

Dragon NaturallySpeaking will add the new words to your vocabulary (marked with a star ✳ in the list). A dialog box appears asking if you want to train the new words now. You should train any words that are not pronounced the way they are spelled.

To train the new words, click Yes and follow the instructions on the screen. For more information, see "Training Dragon NaturallySpeaking to recognize problem words" on page 59.

To skip this step, click No.

5   Click Next to continue.

The Adapt to document style dialog box opens.

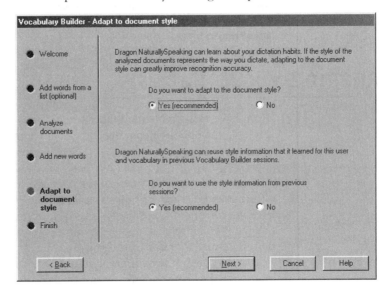

To adapt to document style:

1   For the first option, select "Yes" to have Vocabulary Builder modify your speech files based on the language data gathered in analyzing your documents. If you select "No," the data won't be used. You could select "No" if you were using Vocabulary Builder only to find new words (for example, if you were processing documents you didn't write but which contain words you use).

2 For the second option, select "Yes" to preserve previously gathered language data. If you select "No," this data will be lost. You could select "No" if you wanted to overwrite data gathered previously (for example, if you processed the wrong documents the last time you ran Vocabulary Builder).

> **NOTE** *This option will be dimmed (grayed out) the first time you run Vocabulary Builder, since there are not yet any previous sessions.*

3 Make your selections and click Next to continue.

4 On the final dialog box of Vocabulary Builder, review the summary information and click Finish to save your changes.

> **NOTE** *If you ever make unwanted changes to your speech files when running Vocabulary Builder, you can restore a backup copy of your user. See "Restoring a backup copy of a user" on page 136.*

Managing vocabularies

If you have Dragon NaturallySpeaking Professional or a higher edition, you have the option of creating additional vocabularies with specialized words.

An additional vocabulary can improve recognition accuracy if you have different and distinct writing styles and if the writing you do requires a large vocabulary of specialized terms. For example, a doctor who uses Dragon NaturallySpeaking for dictating medical reports and also for sending e-mail to friends and family may be able to enhance recognition accuracy by having two different vocabularies: a vocabulary for professional writing and one for informal correspondence.

Whether or not you need an additional vocabulary depends on how many words you would need to add to your current vocabulary to make it effective for all the writing you do. Unless this number is greater than 10,000 words (as it might be for a doctor), you should be able to add all the specialized terms you use to your current vocabulary without compromising the recognition accuracy of other words.

Keep in mind that a single vocabulary is easier to maintain. If you have different vocabularies, you may have to add and delete words in multiple places.

Language data gathered when you run Vocabulary Builder is specific to a single vocabulary. But acoustic data—information about how you pronounce different words—applies across vocabularies. When you correct a word in the Quick Correct list or the Correction dialog box, or train it in the Train Words dialog box, Dragon NaturallySpeaking adjusts the acoustic data for that word and all other words with similar sound patterns.

The one case in which acoustic data isn't shared across vocabularies is when a spoken form is added for a word. For example, if you edit the written form of "Laura" to add a spoken form of "Laura my officemate," as in the example on page 43, this pronunciation information is stored in the vocabulary along with the word, so it's specific to a single vocabulary.

You can create, open, delete, rename, import, and export vocabularies in the Manage Vocabularies dialog box. See the next section for details.

Creating vocabularies

This procedure applies only to Dragon NaturallySpeaking Professional and higher editions.

To create a vocabulary:

1 On the NaturallySpeaking menu, point to Advanced and click Manage Vocabularies. The Manage Vocabularies dialog box opens.

2 Click New. Enter a name for the new vocabulary and select a vocabulary on which to base it.

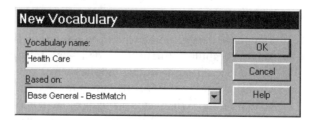

You can base the new vocabulary on one of the standard Dragon NaturallySpeaking vocabularies (which begin with the word "Base") or on one of your current vocabularies.

3 Click OK to create the vocabulary.

4 To start using the new vocabulary, you need to open it first. See the following section, "Opening vocabularies."

5 Run Vocabulary Builder to customize the new vocabulary. See "Building your vocabulary" on page 44.

> **NOTE** *Vocabularies are associated with specific users. If you create an additional vocabulary, it's available only to the current user. However, you can export and import vocabularies to transfer them between users. See "Importing and exporting vocabularies" on page 57.*

Opening vocabularies

This procedure applies only to Dragon NaturallySpeaking Professional and higher editions.

To open a vocabulary:

1 On the NaturallySpeaking menu, point to Advanced and click Manage Vocabularies.

2 Select a vocabulary and click Open.

> **TIP** *You can also open a vocabulary that was open recently. From the NaturallySpeaking menu, point to Advanced and click Open Recent Vocabularies.*

Deleting vocabularies

This procedure applies only to Dragon NaturallySpeaking Professional and higher editions.

To delete a vocabulary:

1 On the NaturallySpeaking menu, point to Advanced and click Manage Vocabularies.

2 Select the vocabulary you want to delete and click Delete.

If you want to delete the open vocabulary, you must close it first by opening a different one.

There must be at least one vocabulary for each user, so if you've got only one, you cannot delete it.

NOTE *Always use the Delete button to delete vocabularies; don't remove folders from the NatSpeak\...\Users folder on your hard disk. Using the Delete button is the only way to properly remove all information about a vocabulary from your computer.*

Renaming vocabularies

This procedure applies only to Dragon NaturallySpeaking Professional and higher editions.

To rename a vocabulary:

1 On the NaturallySpeaking menu, point to Advanced and click Manage Vocabularies.

2 Select a vocabulary and click Rename.

3 In the Rename Vocabulary dialog box, type a new name for the vocabulary and click OK.

4 Click Cancel to close the Open Vocabulary dialog box.

Importing and exporting vocabularies

These procedures apply only to Dragon NaturallySpeaking Professional and higher editions.

Vocabularies are associated with specific users. You can, however, copy vocabularies between users by importing and exporting them. For example, if you create another user for use with a portable recorder, you may want to copy your current vocabulary to the new user. You can do this by exporting the vocabulary from your current first user and then importing it to the new user. The following sections provide instructions.

To export a vocabulary:

1 (optional) Create a folder in which to store the exported vocabulary files. (The folder can be anywhere on your hard disk.)

2 Open the user that has the vocabulary you want to export. Select it from the list in the DragonBar Users menu. Or, point to Users, click Manage Users (to open the dialog box), then select the user you want and click Open.

3 On the NaturallySpeaking menu, point to Advanced and click Manage Vocabularies.

4 Select the vocabulary you want to export and click Export. (You may be prompted to save changes to your speech files.)

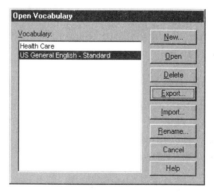

5 Open the folder you created for storing the exported vocabulary files.

6 Click Save.

The exported vocabulary is saved as five files, all with the same name but with different extensions (.TOP, .TO1, .TO2, and so on). These five files must remain in the same folder. When you later import the vocabulary, the file with the extension .TOP (for topic) is the one to select.

To import a vocabulary:

1 Open the user to which you want to import the vocabulary. (On the DragonBar Users menu, click Manage Users. From the Manage Users dialog box, select the user you want and click Open.)

2 On the NaturallySpeaking menu, point to Advanced and click Manage Vocabularies.

3 Click Import and then open the folder that contains the exported vocabulary files. (You can only import vocabularies that have been exported.)

4 Select the vocabulary you want to import by selecting the file with the extension .TOP, and then click Open.

5 In the Import Vocabulary dialog box, enter a name for the imported vocabulary.

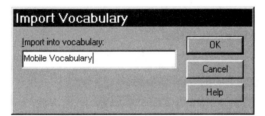

6 Click OK to save the vocabulary.

7 Click Cancel to close the Open Vocabulary dialog box.

Training Dragon NaturallySpeaking to recognize problem words

If Dragon NaturallySpeaking continues to get the same word or phrase wrong, it probably doesn't recognize the way you pronounce it. When this happens, you should teach Dragon NaturallySpeaking how you say it. This is known as *training* the word or phrase.

Training words

Typically, correcting a word is all you need to do for Dragon NaturallySpeaking to get it right the next time. But if you find yourself correcting the same word or phrase over and over, you need to train Dragon NaturallySpeaking to understand it. Training is the most effective way to teach the program your pronunciation.

You can train Dragon NaturallySpeaking after making corrections, after adding a new word, or from Vocabulary Editor. The Train Words dialog box opens when you:

- click the Train... button in the Correction dialog box
- add an individual word, if you select the check box "I want to train the pronunciation of this word"
- click the Train... button in Vocabulary Editor

TIP *You can select more than one word to train in Vocabulary Editor by holding down the CTRL key while you click.*

To train a word:

1 Open the Train Words dialog box to display the word or phrase to train.

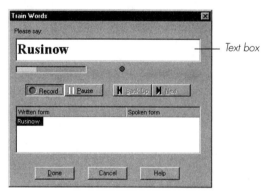

▲ *Train Words helps you teach Dragon NaturallySpeaking your pronunciation for a word or phrase it continues to get wrong.*

2 Click or say "*Record.*"

3 Pronounce the word or phrase.

The text disappears, and if Dragon NaturallySpeaking successfully recognized the word, the dot below the text box lights up briefly. (You may be prompted to say the word more than once.)

NOTE *When you train a word after correcting it in the Correction dialog box, you're prompted to say both the correct and incorrect word. This helps Dragon NaturallySpeaking learn the difference. If both words are pronounced exactly the same (for example, "write" and "right"), there's no need to train either one.*

4 If you want to train the word or phrase again (if you misspoke, for example), click the Record button again and repeat the word or phrase; otherwise, click Done.

You can also train any voice command that Dragon NaturallySpeaking consistently misunderstands.

Training a voice command

If Dragon NaturallySpeaking often gets a specific voice command wrong (for example, it hears *"Correct That"* as *"Correct the"*), you can train it to recognize your pronunciation for the command.

Before you spend time training a command, make sure the phrase you're saying is a real command. Consult the online Help, or check the *Command Quick Reference* card or the Dragon NaturallySpeaking Version 5 Commands List on page 171.

If the command you want to train appears in the following list, you can train it from Vocabulary Editor (these commands are stored as words in the vocabulary):

- New-Line
- New-Paragraph
- Next-Line
- Next-Paragraph
- Cap
- Caps-On
- Caps-Off
- All-Caps
- All-Caps-On

- All-Caps-Off
- No-Caps
- No-Caps-On
- No-Caps-Off
- No-Space
- No-Space-On
- No-Space-Off

To train a command in the previous list:

1 On the NaturallySpeaking menu, point to Advanced, and then click Edit Vocabulary.

2 Scroll to the top of the list where the commands are listed. (To get there quickly, click in the list and press the Home key.)

3 Click the command you want to train. The spoken form won't become highlighted, but the space in the Written form column will.

4 Click Train.

For further instructions, see steps 2–4 beginning on page 60.

TIP *You can select multiple commands to train by holding down the CTRL key while you click. It's a good idea to train any similar-sounding commands at the same time. For example, if you're training "New Paragraph" also train "New Line."*

To train a command that doesn't appear in the list on page 62, follow the procedure below.

To train other commands:

1 On the NaturallySpeaking menu, point to Words and click Train Words.

2 In the Train Words dialog box, type the command you want to train.

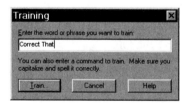

Enter the command with the exact capitalization shown on your *Command Quick Reference* card or in Appendix B of this guide. For example, to train *"Correct That,"* capitalize the words exactly as shown.

3   Click OK.

For further instructions, follow steps 2–4 beginning on page 60.

Running General Training again

If you've been following the procedures in this chapter, but Dragon NaturallySpeaking continues to make a lot of mistakes, you may need to spend some more time teaching the program how you pronounce words. You can do this by running General Training again and reading another training text aloud.

Doing more General Training can also help if your speaking style has changed since your first experience with Dragon NaturallySpeaking. If you spend some more time training the program and make an effort to speak the way you do when you dictate, you should see an improvement in accuracy.

The first time you do additional training, you must read for at least 18 minutes; after that, there is no fixed time limit. You should read at least one complete selection from the General Training texts, until you can click the Finish button. If you click Cancel, your training will be lost.

Even if you're getting good recognition accuracy, consider running General Training again after you've been dictating long enough to have a dictation style (a few weeks). Doing more training can further improve accuracy if your speaking style has changed at all since your first experience. Running General Training again is also a good idea if you move to a noisier environment or change your microphone or sound card.

To run General Training:

1   From the Dragon NaturallySpeaking menu, point to Advanced and click Train User. The General Training dialog box appears.

2   Select the text you want to read (you can select a different text than the one you read the first time) and click Train Now.

3 Follow the instructions on the screen.

TIP *As you read, speak clearly, as if you were dictating the text into a document. This will allow the program to learn how you sound when you dictate.*

4 When you've read as much as you want (or at least one complete text), click Finish.

CHAPTER 4

Dictating Names, Numbers & Punctuation

Your *Quick Start* guide explains the basics of dictating.

This chapter describes how to dictate:

- Names of people, places, and events
- Abbreviations and acronyms
- Hyphenated and compound words
- Words that end with 's
- E-mail and Web addresses
- Special characters (such as é and ¥)
- Foreign words
- Numbers (including telephone numbers and dates)

Dictating names of people, places, and events

Many names of people, places, and events are already in the Dragon NaturallySpeaking vocabulary. For example, you can dictate *"Martin Luther King," "Papua New Guinea,"* and *"Boston, Massachusetts."* Your first step should always be to try dictating the name.

To dictate names:

US/Canada: Dictate your name and your town. For example, say *"My name is Carol Macintosh [period] I live in Chicago [comma] Illinois [period]"*

Other Dialects: Dictate your name and your town. For example, say *"My name is Harriet Timms [full stop] I live in Marlow [comma] Buckinghamshire [full stop]"*

NOTE *All non-US/Canada dialects (UK, Australian, Indian, and Southeast Asian English) use the same commands for punctuation, selection, number formatting, and so on.*

Say the words as clearly as possible. (Dragon NaturallySpeaking automatically capitalizes the names it knows, so you don't have to say *"Cap."*)

Did Dragon NaturallySpeaking get your name and town correct? If not, it may mean that your name, town, or both aren't in the vocabulary. Not all proper names are in the vocabulary, but you can easily add them. See "Quick and easy ways to add new words" on page 34.

When you dictate a name that can be spelled more than one way (for example, "John" or "Jon"), Dragon NaturallySpeaking types the most common spelling. If this isn't the spelling you want, just correct the word (as described in "Correcting recognition mistakes" on page 15). The Correction dialog box displays any alternative spellings that are already in the vocabulary. If none of the choices are what you want, type or spell the name the way you want it to appear.

If the name is a popular one, Dragon NaturallySpeaking may continue to use the more common spelling. If this is a problem, you can create a new *spoken form* in your vocabulary for entering the spelling you want (see "Editing your vocabulary" on page 41). Or, if you never use a particular spelling, you can delete it from the vocabulary.

Dictating abbreviations and acronyms

Dragon NaturallySpeaking knows many common abbreviations (such as NYC and BBC) and acronyms (such as NATO). To dictate an abbreviation or acronym, just say it as you normally would.

TO ENTER	SAY
US/Canada: Dr. Other Dialects: Dr	Doctor
UK	U K *(say each letter)*
RSVP	R S V P *(say each letter)*
HTML	H T M L *(say each letter)*
8 cm	eight centimeters
US/Canada: pp. 27–33 Other Dialects: pp 27–33	pages 27 hyphen 33
NATO	NATO *(say as one word)*
NASDAQ	NASDAQ *(say as one word)*

If Dragon NaturallySpeaking types the full word instead of the abbreviation or acronym or enters the wrong word, just correct it (as described in "Correcting recognition mistakes" on page 15). The Correction dialog box should display the abbreviation or acronym on the list of alternatives. If none of the choices are correct, type it or spell it by voice.

If you want to include periods or full stops in an abbreviation (for example, U. K. instead of UK), just correct it. When the Quick Correct list or Correction dialog box opens, you may see a version that includes periods or full stops. If not, edit the corrected text to include them.

NOTE *If Dragon NaturallySpeaking continues to misrecognize an abbreviation or acronym, it may not be in the vocabulary. If you use it often, you should add it to the vocabulary (as described in "Quick and easy ways to add new words" on page 34).*

Dictating hyphenated words

Many hyphenated words and phrases are already in the Dragon NaturallySpeaking vocabulary. To dictate a word or phrase that's hyphenated based on standard usage, just say it as you normally would.

TO ENTER	SAY
long-lasting	long lasting
up-to-date schedule	up to date schedule
Tokyo-based company	Tokyo based company
nine-year-old boy	nine year old boy

Including hyphens as you dictate

To hyphenate words that Dragon NaturallySpeaking doesn't hyphenate automatically, just say *"hyphen"* wherever you want a hyphen.

TO ENTER	SAY
speech-recognition software	speech [hyphen] recognition software
power-sharing agreement	power [hyphen] sharing agreement
Elizabeth Walker-Smith	Elizabeth Walker [hyphen] Smith

Adding hyphens later

You can hyphenate the last words you said or hyphenate selected words by saying *"Hyphenate That.*

NOTE Commands that act on the last thing you said or on selected text work in the DragonPad, Microsoft Word, and Corel WordPerfect, but not work in all programs. See the online Help Command List, or "Which commands work in which programs?" on page 171.

To add a hyphen:

1 Select the words you want to hyphenate.

For example, if you want to hyphenate "speech recognition" in the following sentence, say *"Select speech recognition."*

I'm using speech recognition software

2 Say *"Hyphenate That."*

This command adds a hyphen between the selected words. To move back to the end of the line, you can say *"Go to End of Line."*

Removing hyphens

You can remove a hyphen by selecting it and replacing it with a space.

To remove a hyphen:

1 Say *"Select hyphen."*

2 Say *"Space Bar."*

Preventing hyphens

You can prevent Dragon NaturallySpeaking from entering a hyphen by pausing where the hyphen would normally be.

For example, to type "long lasting" (normally hyphenated) say *"long,"* then pause for a moment, and then say *"lasting."* Or you can say *"long space-bar lasting"* without pausing, to insert a space in place of the hyphen.

Dictating compound words

Dragon NaturallySpeaking joins compound words (such as "notebook") automatically based on standard usage. To dictate a compound word, just say it as you normally would.

Compounding words as you dictate

To compound words that Dragon NaturallySpeaking doesn't join automatically, just say *"No Space"* between the words.

TO ENTER	SAY
dragonsystems	[No Caps] dragon [No Space] systems
WorldWide Web	[Cap] world [No Space] [Cap] wide [Cap] web

You can also dictate consecutive words without spaces by turning "no spaces" on and then turning them off when you've finished.

To dictate consecutive words without spaces:

1 Say *"No Space On"* to turn no spaces on.

2 Dictate the words you want to appear without spaces.

3 Say *"No Space Off"* to turn no spaces off.

Compounding words later

You can compound the last words you said or compound selected words by saying *"Compound That."**

To compound words:

1 Select the text you want to join. For example, if you want to join the words "Web TV," say *"Select Web TV."*

2 Say *"Compound That."*

This command removes all spaces between selected words. (Any tabs or line breaks are also removed.)

TIP *If the command doesn't work (for example, if the words "compound that" are typed into your document), you may need to say the command more clearly. Say "Undo That" (or press* CTRL+Z) *to undo the last action, and then try the command again. Or you can press the* CTRL *key while dictating to force Dragon NaturallySpeaking to recognize what you say as a command.*

Dictating words that end with 's

When you dictate a word that should end with 's (apostrophe ess), Dragon NaturallySpeaking adds it if it can hear the "ess" sound and if the ending makes sense in the context.

---

* This command works in the DragonPad, Microsoft Word, and Corel WordPerfect, but it doesn't work in all programs. See the online Help Command List, or "Which commands work in which programs?" on page 171.

To dictate a word ending with 's, just say it as you normally would. (For some words, you may need to emphasize the "ess" sound.) If Dragon NaturallySpeaking doesn't include the 's, you can add it later.

TO ENTER	SAY
We took Mary's car	We took Mary's car
that's enough	that's enough
it's time to go	it's time to go

Including 's as you dictate

When you want to make sure that Dragon NaturallySpeaking types a word with 's, just say *"apostrophe ess"* (or *"apostrophe"* for words that already end in s) after saying the word.

TO ENTER	SAY
We took my brother's car	We took my brother [apostrophe ess] car
I met my friends' children	I met my friends [apostrophe] children
Lois's car	Lois [apostrophe ess] car

Adding 's later

You can add 's to a word by selecting it and then saying it again with *"apostrophe ess."*

To add 's later:

1 Select the text to which you want to add 's. For example, say *"Select brothers."*

2 Say the word followed by *"apostrophe ess"* (for example, say *"brother apostrophe ess"*).

This changes "brothers" to "brother's."

Or, you can use the "Insert After" command (see page 88). For example, say *"Insert after brother,"* pause, and then say *""apostrophe ess."*

Dictating e-mail and Web addresses

You can dictate e-mail and Web addresses as you would normally say them. Dragon NaturallySpeaking formats them for you automatically.

TO ENTER	SAY
Virginia@aol.com	[Cap] virginia at a o l dot com
info@dragonsys.com	[No Caps On] info at dragon sys dot com [No Caps Off]
http://www.dragonsystems.com	[No Caps On] h t t p w w w dot dragon systems dot com [No Caps Off]

NOTE *To be able to dictate e-mail and Web addresses as described in this section, you must keep the "Format Web and E-mail addresses automatically" option selected in the Dragon NaturallySpeaking Options dialog box (Formatting tab).*

Here are some guidelines for dictating e-mail and Web addresses:

- When you say *"h t t p," "w w w,"* or *"web,"* Dragon NaturallySpeaking knows to format the next words you say as a Web address.

- Say the following abbreviations by pronouncing them as words: *"co," "com," "edu," "gov," "mil," "net,"* and *"org."*

- Say the following abbreviations by saying each letter: *"a c," "b n," "c a," "c o," "e d u," "h k," "i d," "i n," "j p," "m y," "p h," "s g," "t h,"* and *"u k."*

- Use the *"No Caps On"* and *"No Caps Off"* commands to enter an e-mail or Web address in all lowercase letters. For more information about controlling capitalization, see "Dictating consecutive words in all lowercase letters" on page 97.

If the address you're dictating contains an unusual word (for example, "tiac" or "juno"), Dragon NaturallySpeaking will make mistakes. You should correct the mistake (as described in "Correcting recognition mistakes" on page 15) and train the program to recognize the address (as described in "Training Dragon NaturallySpeaking to recognize problem words" on page 59).

TIP You can create dictation shortcuts for e-mail and Web addresses you use often. See "Creating dictation shortcuts" on page 38.

Dictating special characters

Dictating common special characters

The following special characters are in the Dragon NaturallySpeaking vocabulary. To dictate these characters, just say their names.

TO ENTER	SAY
&	ampersand *or* and-sign
*	asterisk
@	at sign
`	backquote
©	copyright sign
^	caret
°	degree sign
$	dollar sign *or* dollar*
€	euros *or* euro-sign*
%	percent sign
®	registered sign
§	section sign
™	trademark sign
+	plus sign
-	minus sign
«	open euro quote
»	close euro quote
#	**All Dialects:** hash sign *or* sharp sign **US/Canada:** number sign *or* pound sign
£	**US/Canada:** pound sterling sign* **Other Dialects:** pound sign *or* pound

TO ENTER	SAY
:-)	smiley face
:-(	frowny face
;-)	winky face

* For more information about dictating currency in different dialects, see "Currency and coin" on page 81.

For more complete lists of special characters, see "Entering punctuation and special characters" on page 194 or the online Help.

Dictating uncommon special characters

If you use uncommon special characters in your writing (for example, the yen sign ¥), you can also enter them by voice. You must, however, use the Correction dialog box the first time you dictate them, to add them to your vocabulary.

For example, if you want to enter the Japanese currency symbol for yen (¥) into your document, you could dictate *"yen sign"* and then correct the result to be ¥ instead of the words *"yen sign."* The next time you say *"yen sign,"* Dragon NaturallySpeaking should enter the symbol, not the words.

For the complete list of special characters you can enter by using the Correction dialog box, see the following sections in Appendix B:

- "Publishing symbols" on page 178
- "Currency symbols" on page 179
- "Accented and international characters" on page 179
- "Mathematical symbols" on page 181

To dictate an uncommon special character:

1 In a document, dictate the phrase you want to use to enter the special character (for example, say *"yen sign"*). (Make a note of the phrase you use.)

Dragon NaturallySpeaking enters the words into your document. In this example, it would enter "yen sign."

2 Say *"Correct That"* to open the Correction dialog box.

3 Say the name of the special character (for example, say *"yen sign"* to enter ¥).

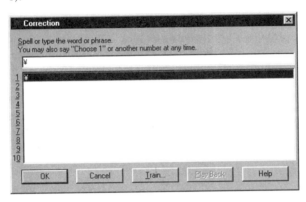

For the complete list of special characters, see page 194 in Appendix B, or the online Help.

4 Click or say *"OK."*

Dragon NaturallySpeaking enters the special character (for example, ¥) and also adds it to the vocabulary. Now when you dictate the phrase (in this example, *"yen sign"*), Dragon NaturallySpeaking should enter the special character, not the words. If the program enters words instead, just correct the mistake (as described in "Correcting recognition mistakes" on page 15). The Correction dialog box should display the special character in the list of alternatives.

Dictating foreign words

Some foreign words that are regularly used in English (such as "laissez-faire") are in the Dragon NaturallySpeaking vocabulary.

If you dictate a foreign word, and Dragon NaturallySpeaking doesn't recognize it, try correcting it. The Correction dialog box may display the word you want on the list of alternatives.

If the foreign word contains an accented character, add it to the vocabulary with the accented character in the written form. See "Adding an individual word" on page 35.

Dictating numbers

You can dictate most numbers as you would normally say them. Many number formats in DragonNaturallySpeaking are controlled by your Windows Regional Settings. To view these settings, point to Settings from the Windows Start menu, click Control Panel, and double-click the Regional Settings icon.

NOTE *If you are having problems dictating numbers, currency, times, or dates, make sure that your Regional Settings match the language (dialect) you selected when you created your user. For more information on choosing a dialect, see your Quick Start guide.*

US/Canada: You can enter $250.95 by saying *"two hundred and fifty dollars and ninety five cents,"* and you can enter 4:05 PM by saying *"four oh five p m."*

Other Dialects: You can enter £250.95 by saying *"two hundred and fifty pounds and ninety five pence,"* and you can enter 4.05 PM by saying *"four oh five p m."*

If you ever have trouble getting Dragon NaturallySpeaking to type a numeral rather than a word (for example, "4" instead of "four"), just say *"numeral"* before saying the number. For example, say *"numeral four."* This forces the program to enter the number as a numeral.

NOTE *To be able to dictate numbers as described in the following sections, you must keep the "Automatically format telephone numbers, currency, times, and other numbers" option selected in the Formatting tab of the Options dialog box.*

Numerals

You can dictate most numerals, including ZIP codes and other numeric postal codes, as you would normally say them.

TO ENTER	SAY
1	one *or* numeral one
5	five *or* numeral five
17	seventeen
23	twenty three
179	one hundred seventy nine *or* one seventy nine

TO ENTER	SAY
5423	five thousand four hundred and twenty three
5,423	five [comma] four twenty three
12,537	twelve thousand five hundred and thirty seven
142,015	one hundred and forty two thousand and fifteen
35.23	thirty five [point] two three
0.03	**All Dialects:** zero [point] zero three **Outside US/Canada:** nought [point] nought three
43.28%	forty three [point] twenty eight [percent sign]
02460	oh two four six zero
02460-1458	oh two four six zero [hyphen] one four five eight

Dragon NaturallySpeaking automatically includes a numeric comma (a comma without a trailing space) in numbers with five or more digits (for example, 12,537). To include a comma in a four-digit number, you must say *"comma."*

NOTE *Dragon NaturallySpeaking uses the decimal separator (dot or comma) and the digit grouping symbol specified in your Regional Settings in the Windows Control Panel.*

Changing the format of a number

If Dragon NaturallySpeaking enters a number in a format you don't want, you can use voice commands to convert it to a numeral or to spell it out.

For example, you can change "seven dollars" to "$7" (**US/Canada**) or "seven pounds" to "£ 7" (**Other Dialects**) by saying *"Format That Number."*

And you can change "$7" to "seven dollars" (**US/Canada**) or "£ 7" to "seven pounds" (**Other Dialects**) by saying *"Format That Spelled Out."*

These commands change the last number dictated or a selected number.

SAY	TO CHANGE
Format That Number	one *to* 1 first *to* 1st twenty-fifth *to* 25th 5 million *to* 5,000,000 five million *to* 5,000,000 **US/Canada:** eight dollars *to* $8 **Other Dialects:** seven pounds *to* £7
Format That Spelled Out	4th *to* fourth 27 *to* twenty-seven 5,000,000 *to* five million
Start Numbers Mode/ Numbers Mode On	Tell Dragon NaturallySpeaking to recognize all your dictation as numbers, typed as numerals.
Stop Numbers Mode/ Numbers Mode Off	Resume normal dictation of text and numbers.

NOTE *The "Format That Number" and "Format That Spelled Out" commands work for numerals and currency, but not for dates, times of day, telephone numbers, and most fractions.*

Using Numbers Mode

Any time you need to dictate a series of numbers and do not want Dragon NaturallySpeaking to recognize them as words, you can turn on Numbers Mode. This could be useful, for example, if you are dictating in a speadsheet program, such as Microsoft Excel®.

To turn Numbers Mode on and off:

1 From the NaturallySpeaking menu, point to Words and then click Numbers Mode. You can also say "*Start Numbers Mode*" or "*Numbers Mode On.*"

A check appears beside the menu command to indicate that Numbers Mode is on.

2 Click Numbers Mode again. You can also say "*Stop Numbers Mode*" or "*Numbers Mode Off.*"

The check disappears, indicating that Numbers Mode is off.

NOTE *With Numbers Mode on, Dragon NaturallySpeaking tries to interpret everything as a number. If you dictate words, the results will be unpredictable. However, you can still navigate menus and switch between programs by voice when Numbers Mode is on.*

Dates

You can dictate most dates the way you would normally say them. Say *"oh"* or *"zero"* to enter 0. In dialects outside US/Canada, you can also say *"nought."*

TO ENTER	SAY
22 January 1999	Twenty two January nineteen ninety nine
April 9, 2001	April 9 [comma] two thousand and one
14/07/85	fourteen [slash] oh seven [slash] eighty five
3/11/02	three [slash] eleven [slash] zero two
3/11/2002	three [slash] eleven [slash] two thousand and two
April 1st	April first
March 22nd	March twenty second
The 1980s	The nineteen eighties

If Dragon NaturallySpeaking types the date in the wrong format, just correct it (as described in "Correcting recognition mistakes" on page 15). When the Correction dialog box opens, the format you want may be on the list of alternatives.

Times of day

US/Canada: Usually, you can dictate the time of day the way you would normally say it. Say *"o'clock"* to enter :00. Dragon NaturallySpeaking automatically types the colon (:) if you say *"a m," "p m,"* or *"o'clock"* when dictating the time. Otherwise, say *"colon zero zero"* to enter :00.

TO ENTER	SAY
8:30	eight [colon] thirty
4:45 AM	four forty five a m
10:22 PM	ten twenty two p m
3:00	three o'clock
5:00 PM	five o'clock p m

Other Dialects: Usually, you can dictate the time of day the way you would normally say it. Say *"o'clock"* to enter .00. Dragon NaturallySpeaking automatically types the point (.) if you say *"a m," "p m,"* or *"o'clock"* when dictating the time. Otherwise, say *"point zero zero"* to enter .00.

TO ENTER	SAY
8.30	eight [colon] thirty
4.45 AM	four forty five a m
10.22 PM	ten twenty two p m
3.00	three o'clock
5.00 PM	five o'clock p m

NOTE *Dragon NaturallySpeaking uses the time separator (dot or colon) and the AM/PM symbol specified in your Regional Settings in the Windows Control Panel.*

Telephone numbers

North American phone numbers
You can say U.S. and Canadian phone numbers (of 7, 10, or 11 digits) naturally, by pausing briefly between each group of numbers. You don't need to dictate hyphens between groups of of 7, 10, or 11 digits. However, when dictating eight-digit numbers starting with 0 or 1 (for example, *1-965-5200*), you must say all the punctuation, including the hyphens, spaces, and brackets.

TO ENTER	SAY
965-5200	nine six five fifty two hundred
617-965-5200	six one seven nine six five fifty two hundred
1-800-555-1212	one eight hundred five five five one two one two
(617) 965-5200	[open parenthesis] six one seven [close parenthesis] nine six five five two hundred
1-212-555-1212	one two one two five five five one two one two

Telephone numbers outside North America

To dictate other phone numbers, including European phone numbers, you must say all the punctuation, including the hyphens, spaces, and parentheses.

TO ENTER	SAY
(01628) 894150	[open parenthesis] oh one six two eight [close parenthesis] space bar eight nine four one five oh
027 629 8944	oh two seven [space bar] six two nine [space bar] eight nine four four
61-7-4695-2055	six one [hyphen] seven [hyphen] four six nine five [hyphen] two zero five five
(65) 2778590	[open parenthesis] six five [close parenthesis] two seven seven eight five nine zero

TIP *In dialects outside US/Canada, you can say "bracket" instead of "parenthesis."*

Currency and coin

You can dictate your own currency as you would normally say it.

Currency in US/Canada (US English dialect)

TO ENTER	SAY
$58.00	fifty eight dollars and zero cents
$1.75	one dollar and seventy five cents
$5.25	five dollars and twenty five cents
$3.9 billion	three point nine billion dollars
£ 45	pound sterling sign forty five
£ 99.50	pound sterling sign ninety-nine point five oh
£ 2.20	pound sterling sign two point two oh
£ 5 million	pound sterling sign five million

Currency in Other Dialects (UK, Australian, Indian, and Southeast Asian English)

TO ENTER	SAY
$58.00	fifty eight dollars
$1.75	one dollar and seventy five cents
$4.25	four dollars twenty five
$3.9 billion	three point nine billion dollars
£ 45	forty five pounds
£ 99.50	ninety nine pounds and fifty pence
£ 2.20	two pounds twenty
£ 5 million	five million pounds

NOTE *Dragon NaturallySpeaking uses the currency symbol ($, £, and so on) specified in your Windows Regional Settings as your default currency.*

Dictate other currencies by first saying the currency symbol followed by the digits.

US/Canada: If your Regional Settings are set to the United States or Canada, your default currency is $ (dollar). If you want to dictate a dollar currency amount, dictate it the way you normally do. If you want to dictate a pound sterling currency amount, say, for example, "*pound sterling sign fifty eight*" (to enter £ 58), and so on.

TIP *In US/Canada, you must say "pound sterling sign" to enter £, since "pound sign" means # in the U.S. vocabulary. In all other dialects, you can say "pound sign" to type £.*

Other Dialects: If your Regional Settings are set to the United Kingdom, your default currency is £ (pound sterling). If you want to dictate a pound sterling currency amount, dictate it the way you normally do. If you want to dictate a dollar currency amount, say, for example, "*dollar sign fifty eight*" (to enter $58) and so on.

NOTE *Australian users can say "fifty eight dollars" to dictate $58, since the Australian default currency is $ in Windows Regional Settings.*

Fractions

You can dictate most common fractions the way you would normally say them. To dictate 1/2, 1/3, 1/4, 1/5, 1/6, 1/7, 1/8, 1/9, 1/10, and 1/16 or a multiple of these fractions, just say the fraction normally.

TO ENTER	SAY
1/2	one half
1/4	one fourth *or* one quarter
15/16	fifteen sixteenths *or* fifteen over sixteen
3 7/8	three and seven eighths *or* three and seven over eight

If Dragon NaturallySpeaking types the fraction as a word (for example, "one-third"), you can correct it as described in "Correcting recognition mistakes" on page 15.

If the denominator is greater than 10, you can enter the fraction by saying "*slash*" or "*over*" between the two numbers.

TO ENTER	SAY
9/12	nine [slash] twelve *or* nine over twelve
5 3/56	five [space bar] three [slash] fifty six
130/70	one thirty over seventy

For information about dictating fraction characters (¼, ½, ¾), see "Dictating uncommon special characters" on page 74.

Roman numerals

You can dictate Roman numerals by saying *"Roman"* and the number. For large numbers, say the number in small combinations (as in the last three examples).

TO ENTER	SAY
I	Roman one
IV	Roman four
V	Roman five
X	Roman ten
L	Roman fifty
C	Roman one hundred
D	Roman five hundred
M	Roman one thousand
XXIV	Roman twenty Roman four
XXXI	Roman thirty Roman one
MCMXCVII	Roman one thousand Roman nine hundred Roman ninety Roman seven

TIP *Don't pause after the word "Roman" when you're dictating a Roman numeral. If you pause, Dragon NaturallySpeaking may enter "Roman three" instead of "III" (for example).*

Postal and Zip Codes

US Zip Codes
You can dictate US five-digit ZIP codes just as you dictate any group of numbers. You must say the hyphen when dictating nine-digit ZIP codes.

UK and Canadian Postal Codes
You can dictate UK postcodes by saying "*Postcode*" followed by the letters and numbers that make up the postcode. For Canadian postal codes, say "*Postal code*" followed by the letters and numbers that make up the postal code. Spacing and formatting will happen automatically.

TO ENTER	SAY
NG3 2HX	Postcode n g three two h x
E10 7BD	Postcode e ten seven b d
EC2Y 4LK	Postcode e c two y four l k
K1A 0M5	Postal code k one a zero m five
X0A 0H0	Postal code x oh a oh h o

CHAPTER **5**

Editing and Revising Text

If you followed the online Tutorial and the *Quick Start* guide, you learned a few useful commands for editing a document by voice.

You learned how to use *Select-and-Say* to revise text, move to the top and bottom of your document, capitalize a word, and apply bold, italics, and underlining.

This chapter describes other ways to edit and revise text in a document by voice. It explains how to:

■   Move around in a document

■   Select text

■   Copy, cut, and paste text

■   Capitalize text

■   Format text

■   Delete text

Selection, capitalization, and formatting commands may work differently in different programs, or be unavailable in some programs. All the commands listed here work in the DragonPad, Microsoft Word, Corel WordPerfect, and WordPad. For more information, see "Which commands work in which programs?" on page 171 of Appendix B.

TIP *If a command doesn't seem to be working, check the DragonBar for a helpful tip or view the Command List of the online Help.*

Moving around in a document

When you're editing a document, you can move around the page by voice. After you place the insertion point where you want it, you can dictate more text, select text, copy and paste, or apply formatting.

Going to the top or bottom of a page or document

You can move to the top or bottom of the current page by saying *"Page Up"* (equivalent to pressing the PAGE UP key) or *"Page Down"* (equivalent to pressing the PAGE DOWN key).

You can move to the top or bottom of your document by saying *"Go to Top"* or *"Go to Bottom."*

You can use any command from the list below:

SAY	THEN (one)
Go to	Top
Move to	Bottom
	Top of Document
	Beginning of Document
	Start of Document
	Bottom of Document

Going to the beginning or end of a line

You can move to the beginning or end of the current line by saying *"Go to Beginning of Line"* or *"Go to End of Line."*

You can use any command from the list below:

SAY	THEN (one)
Go to	Beginning of Line
Move to	Start of Line
	End of Line

Placing the insertion point before or after a specific word

You can place the insertion point before a specific word by saying *"Insert Before"* and then the word or words. You can place the insertion point after a word by saying *"Insert After"* and then the word or words.

After you move the insertion point where you want it, you can dictate more text, paste text, add punctuation, and so on.

To place the insertion point before a specific word:

To move the insertion point before the word "lets" in the sentence below, say *"Insert Before lets"* (or *"Insert Before lets me talk"*). Remember not to pause between any of the words.

Dragon NaturallySpeaking |lets me talk instead of type.

To place the insertion point after a specific word:

To move the insertion point after the word "talk" in the sentence below, say *"Insert After talk"* (or *"Insert After lets me talk"*).

Dragon NaturallySpeaking lets me talk| instead of type.

Moving up or down a paragraph or line

You can move up or down a paragraph by saying *"Move Up a Paragraph"* or *"Move Down a Paragraph."* You can also move up and down a number of paragraphs (up to 20). For example, you can say *"Move Up 3 Paragraphs."*

You can move up or down a line by saying *"Move Up a Line"* or *"Move Down a Line."* You can also move up and down a number of lines (up to 20). For example, you can say *"Move Down 3 Lines."*

See the complete list below:

SAY	THEN *(one)*	THEN *(one)*
Move	Up	a Paragraph *or* 1 Paragraph
	Back	2 Paragraphs
	Down	3 Paragraphs
	Forward	2...20 Paragraphs
		a Line *or* 1 Line
		2 Lines
		3 Lines
		2...20 Lines

Moving right or left a word or character

You can move right or left a word by saying *"Move Right a Word"* or *"Move Left a Word."* You can also move right or left a number of words (up to 20). For example, you can say *"Move Right 3 Words."*

You can move to the next or previous character by saying *"Move Right a Character"* or *"Move Left a Character."* You can also move forward and backward a number of characters (up to 20). For example, you can say *"Move Left 4 Characters."*

See the complete list below:

SAY	THEN (one)	THEN (one)
Move	Right	a Word *or* 1 Word
	Forward	2 Words
	Left	4 Words
	Back	2...20 Words
		a Character *or* 1 Character
		2 Characters
		4 Characters
		2...20 Characters

Selecting text

Using Select-and-Say

You can revise your dictation without correcting it by selecting the text using the *"Select"* command and then saying new words to replace the selected text.

Important!

When text is selected, be careful not to breathe loudly, clear your throat, or make other sounds. Dragon NaturallySpeaking may interpret such noises as speech and replace the selection with new text. If this happens, say *"Undo That"* right away to reverse the action.

To Select-and-Say:

1 Dictate the sentence below:

US/Canada: **Let's meet for lunch on Tuesday [period]**

Other Dialects: **Let's meet for lunch on Tuesday [full stop]**

2 Say *"Select lunch on Tuesday."* The words "lunch on Tuesday" should be highlighted on the screen.

3 Say *"dinner on Wednesday."* These words should replace "lunch on Tuesday."

You can also select punctuation marks.

4 Say: *"Select period"* (**US/Canada**) or *"Select full stop"* (**Other Dialects**). If there's more than one period or full stop, you can say *"Select Again"* to select a different one.

5 To replace the period or full stop with an exclamation mark, say *"exclamation mark."*

> **TIP** *It is often easier for Dragon NaturallySpeaking to find the matching text if you select a short phrase rather than selecting individual words. If you select some words that are already correct, just say them again along with the ones you want to change.*

Selecting the same text again

If the words you're trying to select appear more than once on the screen, and Dragon NaturallySpeaking selects the wrong ones, just say *"Select Again."*

The program then looks for another instance of the same word or words. It always searches backward from where you are. If the program reaches the top of the document while searching backward, it will wrap to the bottom of the document and continue searching backward for the next instance of the text.

> **TIP** *If you want the program to always search forward, you can change this setting. On the NaturallySpeaking menu, point to Advanced, click Options, and then click the Correction tab. Clear the "Select searches backwards" check box.*

You can also say *"Select Again"* if Dragon NaturallySpeaking selects a word that sounds like but is not the word you want (for example, "two" instead of "too").

Unselecting words

If the wrong text is selected, say *"Unselect That."*

You can also "unselect" words by moving your insertion point (by mouse or voice) to another part of your document. For example, say *"Go to End of Line"* or click somewhere else in your document.

A third way to unselect words is to use the *"Select"* command to select different text.

Selecting a longer phrase

You can select a longer phrase for correction by saying *"Select [text] Through [text]"* (**US/Canada**) or *"Select [text] To [text]"* (**Other Dialects**). For [text], substitute the actual word or words at the beginning and the end of the range of wrong words. If the phrase was the last thing you said, you can just say *"Select That."*

Is "That" Too Much?

Saying *"Select That," "Spell That,"* or *"Correct That"* to correct your last phrase is practical only when the phrase contains up to 5 words or 50 characters. A much longer phrase may not fit completely in the Quick Correct list, or even in the Correction dialog box, and it's more difficult to find a correct alternative in the vocabulary lists for a long phrase.

To fix mistakes in a long phrase or sentence, it is best to correct just the specific wrong words using the techniques discussed in this section.

Once the phrase is selected, you can edit and correct it in the Correction dialog box.

NOTE *If you're correcting more than one word, the words must all be in sequence (next to each other). You can't use a single command to correct words that are in different parts of your document.*

To correct a longer phrase:

1 Select the phrase by saying *"Select [text] Through [text]"* (**US/Canada**) or *"Select [text] To [text]"* (**Other Dialects**). For [text], substitute the actual word or words at the beginning and the end of the range of wrong words (they must be visible on the screen).

For example, you could correct the underlined words in the following sentence...

With a little practice, <u>who will develop a habit of dictating an unclear,</u> steady voice, and the computer will understand you better.

...by saying:

(**US/Canada**) *"Select who Through unclear"* or *"Select who will Through an unclear"*

(**Other Dialects**) *"Select who To unclear"* or *"Select who will To an unclear"*

2 (in the DragonPad) If the Quick Correct list appears, look to see if it contains the word or phrase you want. If you see the right word or phrase, choose it from the list as described on page 16, "Correcting mistakes with Quick Correct."

3 If you don't see what you want in the list, or if you don't see the Quick Correct list at all, say *"Spell That"* or *"Correct That."* The Correction dialog box will open.

4 In the Correction dialog box, spell or type the correct words (in this example, *"you will develop the habit of dictating in a clear"*).

5 When you're finished, click or say *"OK."*

The Correction dialog box closes and the text is entered into your document. The insertion point returns to where it was before you made the correction.

Selecting your whole document

You can select all the text in your document by saying *"Select Document"* or *"Select All."* This command is useful when you want to change the font or the way text is aligned.

When you want to copy all the text in a document to another window, the easiest way to do it is with the *"Copy All to Clipboard"* command. (See "Copying text to other programs" on page 106.)

NOTE *The "Scratch That" and "Cut That" commands don't work, nor can you dictate, when a lot of text is selected. This prevents you from accidentally deleting a large part of your document. To remove a large selection, you can say "Delete That" instead.*

Selecting an entire paragraph or line

You can select the current paragraph by saying *"Select Paragraph."* To select the current line, say *"Select Line."*

You can also select a number of paragraphs or lines (up to 20). For example, you can say *"Select Previous 5 Paragraphs."* See the complete list below:

SAY	THEN (one)	THEN (one)
Select	Next	Paragraph
	Previous	2 Paragraphs
	Forward	2...20 Paragraphs
	Back	Line
	Last	2 Lines
		2...20 Lines

Selecting a word or character

You can select the current word by saying *"Select Word."* To select a character, say *"Select Next Character"* or *"Select Previous Character."*

You can also select a number of words or characters (up to 20). For example, say *"Select Previous 2 Words."* See the complete list below:

SAY	THEN (one)	THEN (one)
Select	Next	Word
	Previous	Character
	Forward	2 Words
	Back	4 Characters
	Last	2...20 Words
		2...20 Characters

Copying, cutting, and pasting text

You can move text from one place to another by using the *"Copy That,"* *"Cut That,"* and *"Paste That"* commands.

To copy, cut, or paste text:

1 Select the text you want to copy or cut.

2 Say *"Copy That"* or *"Cut That."*

3 Move the insertion point to where you want to paste the text.

4 Say *"Paste That."*

> **NOTE** *You can copy your entire document to the Clipboard by saying "Copy All to Clipboard." This is useful when you want to copy text to another window. (See "Copying text to other programs" on page 106.)*

Capitalizing text

Capitalizing the first letter of the next word you dictate

Dragon NaturallySpeaking capitalizes many words automatically. It capitalizes the first word in a sentence (following a period, question mark, or exclamation mark). It capitalizes the first word after you say *"New Paragraph"* (though not when you say *"New Line"*), and it capitalizes proper names (when these words are already in the Dragon NaturallySpeaking vocabulary in capitalized form).

When you're dictating, you can capitalize words that aren't automatically capitalized by saying *"Cap"* and then the word. For example, say *"Cap fluffy"* to get "Fluffy."

If you need to dictate the word "cap" in a sentence (as in, "The company is putting a cap on salary increases"), just pause after saying *"cap."*

NOTE *Dragon NaturallySpeaking should capitalize correctly whenever you're dictating in the DragonPad or any of the programs listed on page 171. In other programs, it may not always capitalize the first word you say automatically; you may need to capitalize as you dictate.*

Capitalizing consecutive words

When you want to capitalize consecutive words (for example, if you're dictating a book title), you can turn capitals on and then turn them off when you're finished. This is usually easier than saying *"Cap"* before each word.

To capitalize consecutive words:

1   Say *"Caps On"* to turn capitals on.

NOTE *When "Caps On" is active, Dragon NaturallySpeaking uses title case. This means it capitalizes all words except for articles and prepositions (such as "the" and "to").*

2   Dictate the words you want capitalized. For example, say *"success is a journey [colon] seven steps to achieving success in the business of life."*

Dragon NaturallySpeaking types: "Success Is a Journey: Seven Steps to Achieving Success in the Business of Life."

3   Say *"Caps Off"* to turn capitals off.

Dictating the next word in all capital letters

When you're dictating, you can enter a word in all capital letters by saying *"All Caps"* and then the word.

For example, say *"All Caps please"* to get "PLEASE."

Dictating consecutive words in all capital letters

When you want to dictate consecutive words in all capitals, you can turn all capitals on and then turn them off when you've finished.

To dictate consecutive words in all capitals:

1 Say *"All Caps On"* to turn all capitals on (like pressing the CAPS LOCK key).

2 Dictate the words you want to appear in all caps.

3 Say *"All Caps Off"* to turn all capitals off.

Dictating the next word in all lowercase letters

When you're dictating, you can enter a word in all lowercase letters by saying *"No Caps"* and then the word.

For example, say *"No Caps jack"* to get "jack." (Dragon NaturallySpeaking normally capitalizes this and other proper names.)

Dictating consecutive words in all lowercase letters

When you want to dictate consecutive words in lowercase letters (for example, names of computer files or e-mail addresses), you can turn the "no-capitals" feature on and then turn it off when you are finished. This is usually easier than saying *"No Caps"* before each word.

To dictate consecutive words in all lowercase letters:

1 Say *"No Caps On"* to turn no capitals on.

2 Dictate the words you want to appear in all lowercase.

3 Say *"No Caps Off"* to turn no capitals off.

Capitalizing (or uncapitalizing) text already in your document

You can change the capitalization of text already in your document by selecting it and then saying *"Cap That," "All Caps That,"* or *"No Caps That."*

To capitalize or uncapitalize text:

1 Select the text you want to change.

2 Say *"Cap That," "All Caps That,"* or *"No Caps That."*

Formatting text

In the DragonPad, Microsoft Word, Corel WordPerfect and WordPad, you can use commands to specify any combination of font name, size, and style, in that order. These commands change text you dictate from then on, or text you have selected.

To set a new style for text you are about to dictate, use the *"Set Font"* and *"Set Size"* commands. To change text you have already dictated, or text you select, use the *"Format That"* command. You can also select text and apply (or remove) bold, italics, underline, or strikeout formats, or change the alignment of text.

Changing the font as you dictate

When you're dictating, you can change the font face, size, and style by saying *"Set Font"* followed by the font attributes you want.

For example, you can say *"Set Font Times"* or *"Set Font Arial 12 Bold."* When you continue dictating, the new text appears with the font attributes you set.

Changing font face

SAY	THEN (one)
Set Font	Times
	Times New Roman
	Arial
	Courier
	Courier New

Changing font size

Say *"Set Size"* and then a size from 4 to 100 points (or 120 points). For example, say *"Set Size 18."* Then, continue dictating.

Changing font style

SAY	THEN *(one)*
Set Font	Bold
	Italics
	Underline
	Strikeout
	Plain *or* Plain Text *or* Normal *or* Regular

Changing a combination of font face, size, and style
Say *"Set Font"* and then the attributes you want (listed in the previous sections). You can specify any combination of face, size, and style, but you must specify these attributes in that order (face, then size, then style). See the list of examples below:

■ *"Set Font Arial"*

■ *"Set Font Arial 12"* or *"Set Font Arial 12 Point"*

■ *"Set Size 12 Bold"*

■ *"Set Font Arial Bold"*

■ *"Set Font Bold"*

NOTE *If you're changing only the font size, use the "Set Size" commands, not the "Set Font" command.*

Changing the font later

You can go back and change the font face, size, or style of text by selecting it and then using the *"Format That"* commands. *"Format That"* works on selected text, or the last thing you said, with the same combinations of font face, size, and style as the *"Set Font"* commands in the tables from the previous section.

To change the font:

1 Select the text you want to change.

2 Say *"Format That"* and then the font attributes you want to apply as described in the previous section.

Adding (or removing) bold, italics, and underlining

You can apply formatting to text in your document by selecting it and then saying *"Bold That," "Italicize That,"* or *"Underline That."* You can also say *"Strikeout That."*

To add bold, italics, and underlining:

1 Select the text you want to change.

2 Say *"Bold That," "Italicize That," Underline That,"* or *"Strikeout That."*

To remove formatting:

1 Select the text you want to change.

2 Say *"Restore That"* to remove formatting.

Aligning text

You can change how text is aligned by placing your insertion point in the text and saying *"Center That," "Left Align That,"* or *"Right Align That."*

To align text:

1 Move the insertion point to the text you want to align.

2 Say *"Center That," "Left Align That,"* or *"Right Align That."*

You can also use the following commands on the last thing you said or on selected text: *"Format That Centered," "Format That Left Aligned,"* and *"Format That Right Aligned."*

Deleting text

Deleting the last words you dictated

You can erase the last words you dictated by saying *"Scratch That"* or *"Delete That."* When you say either command, Dragon NaturallySpeaking erases the last thing it typed into your document. This may be a full sentence, a phrase, or just one word, if that's all you said before pausing.

You can say *"Scratch That"* (but not *"Delete That"*) up to ten times to delete the last few things you said. If you repeat the command, you must pause before saying it again. You can also say, for example, *"Scratch That 5 Times."*

Backing up as you dictate

When you're dictating, sometimes you may hesitate or think of a better way to say something right after you've said it. When this happens, you can use the *"Resume With"* command to back up to where you were before the mistake.

Just say *"Resume With"* immediately followed by the word or words you want to back up to. Then, continue dictating. Any text after the new insertion point will be replaced with your new dictation.

NOTE *When using the "Resume With" command, remember not to pause in the middle. Say "Resume With" and then immediately say the words you want to back up to. These words must be in the last three or four sentences (100 characters) you said; you can't use "Resume With" to back up to an earlier part of your document.*

To back up as you dictate:

1 Suppose you dictate this sentence: *"I have a deadline this week, but we could meet for lunch... um... er... next Wednesday."*

2 To correct the sentence, back up to the last correct words you remember dictating. For example, say *"Resume With meet for lunch."* (Remember not to pause in the middle.)

3 Then, dictate the rest of the sentence. For example, say *"next Wednesday at noon."*

Deleting specific words

You can delete text by selecting it and saying *"Delete That."*

To delete text:

1 Select the text you want to delete.

2 Say *"Delete That."*

You can also say *"Scratch That"* to do the same thing.

Deleting the next or previous paragraph or line

You can delete the next or previous paragraph by saying *"Delete Next Paragraph"* or *"Delete Previous Paragraph."* You can delete the next or previous line by saying *"Delete Next Line"* or *"Delete Previous Line."*

You can also delete a number of paragraphs or lines (up to 20). For example, you can say *"Delete Previous 5 Paragraphs."* See the complete list below:

SAY	THEN (one)	THEN (one)
Delete	Next	Paragraph
	Previous	2 Paragraphs
	Forward	2...20 Paragraphs
	Back	Line
	Last	2 Lines
		2...20 Lines

Deleting the next or previous word or character

You can delete the next or previous word by saying *"Delete Next Word"* or *"Delete Previous Word."* You can delete the next or previous character by saying *"Delete Next Character"* or *"Delete Previous Character."*

You can also delete a number of words or characters (up to 20). For example, you can say *"Delete Previous 5 Words."* See the complete list below:

SAY	THEN (one)	THEN (one)
Delete	Next	Word
	Forward	2 Words
	Previous	2...20 Words
	Back	Character
	Last	4 Characters
		2...20 Characters

NOTE *Another way to delete the previous character is by saying "Backspace." This is equivalent to pressing the BACKSPACE key. You can "press" it multiple times (up to 20) by saying, for example, "Backspace 5."*

CHAPTER 6

Working With Your Desktop and Windows

In the previous chapters, you learned how to use Dragon NaturallySpeaking to enter text.

You can also use Dragon NaturallySpeaking to control your computer. For example, you can start programs, open menus, and click buttons by using your voice rather than the mouse and keyboard.

This chapter describes how to:

- Start programs
- Open documents and folders
- Switch between open windows
- Copy text to other programs
- Open and close menus
- Select buttons, tabs, and options
- Select icons on the desktop
- Resize and close windows
- Scroll in windows and list boxes
- Press keyboard keys
- Move the mouse pointer and click the mouse

You can start and control most programs by voice. (If you can't control a particular program by voice, it's probably not designed for "hands-free" use.) If you're using Windows NT®, you will need Service Pack 6 or later to use the voice commands described in this chapter.

Active Accessibility is required to control Microsoft Office 97 and Office 2000 (including Microsoft Word, Excel, PowerPoint, Outlook, and

Microsoft Access), Windows Explorer, and Internet Explorer. From the NaturallySpeaking menu, select Advanced, then click Options. Click the Miscellaneous tab and make sure that "Active Accessibility for menu and dialog control" is selected.

Starting programs

You can use voice commands to start a program that appears anywhere on your Windows Start menu or desktop. You can't start Dragon NaturallySpeaking by voice, because the program has to be running before it can hear you.

Starting a program from the Start menu

To start a program from the Start menu, say *"Start"* and then the name of the program exactly as it appears on the menu or submenu (it doesn't have to be visible). For example, to start Internet Explorer, say *"Start Internet Explorer."*

To start a program:

1 Make sure Dragon NaturallySpeaking is running and the microphone is on.

2 Say *"Start"* and then the name of the program. For example, say *"Start WordPad."*

> **NOTE** *To start certain Windows utilities, you must open and navigate the Start menu (see "Opening and closing menus" on page 107). These utilities are Shut Down, Log Off, Help, Run, Favorites, Find, and Settings.*

Starting a program from the Windows desktop

To start a program on your Windows desktop, just say *"Start"* and then the name below the icon. For example, to start Internet Explorer, say *"Start Internet Explorer."*

Internet
Explorer ———— *Say "Start Internet Explorer"*

TIP *You can also open other desktop items with the "Start" command. For example, you can say "Start My Computer."*

Opening documents and folders

You can use voice commands to open a document or folder that appears on your Windows Start menu or desktop.

Opening documents and folders from the Start menu

To open a document or folder from the Start menu, say *"Start"* and then the name of the document or folder exactly as it appears on the menu.

For example, to open a document named SALES.DOC, you could say *"Start Sales dot doc."* To open a document named JOURNAL.WPD, you could say *"Start journal dot w p d."*

If the document doesn't open, but the Results box shows that your command was recognized correctly, make sure the file you're trying to open is still on your computer.

Opening documents and folders from the Windows desktop

To open a document or folder from your Windows desktop, just say *"Start"* and then the name below the icon. For example, to open a folder named "Projects," say *"Start Projects."*

Projects ——— *Say "Start Projects"*

Switching between open windows

You can switch between the windows you have open by saying *"Switch to"* and then say the name of the program or document window exactly as it appears in the title bar.

For example, if Lotus Notes is running, you can switch to it by saying *"Switch to Lotus Notes."*

Say *"Switch to Lotus Notes"*

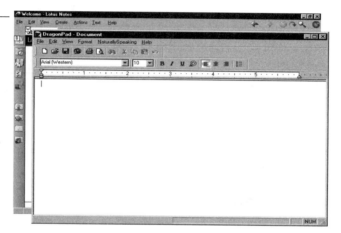

You can also switch between open windows by saying *"Switch to Previous Window"* (same as pressing ALT+TAB) and *"Switch to Next Window"* (same as pressing ALT+SHIFT+TAB).

You can switch to the DragonPad by saying *"Switch to NaturallySpeaking"* or *"Switch to DragonPad."*

Copying text to other programs

When you've finished dictating, you can copy your text to another window. For example, if you dictate a message in Microsoft Word, you can then copy it to Microsoft Outlook.

To copy text to another program:

1 Say *"Copy All to Clipboard"* to copy your entire document.

2 Switch to another program, such as Microsoft Outlook (as described in the previous section, "Switching between open windows").

3 Say *"Paste That."*

4 To return to Microsoft Word, say *"Switch to Microsoft Word"* or *"Switch to Previous Window"* as described in the previous section.

Opening and closing menus

When Dragon NaturallySpeaking is running, you can activate any menu by saying its name.

To open a menu:

1 Open a program window (for example, Microsoft Word) and make it active.

Say the name of the menu you want to open (for example, say *"File"*). If the command does not work, try saying *"Click"* and then the name of the menu you want to open (for example, say *"Click File"*).

Say "File or
"Click File"

Say "Save"

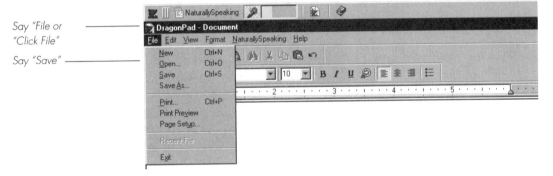

2 In this example, the File menu should open. If the command doesn't work (for example, if the word "click" is typed into your document), you may have paused in the middle of the command.

3 Say the name of a menu item to activate it (for example, say *"Save"*).

You must say any punctuation mark or special character included in the menu. For example, to open a menu named Undo/Redo, say *"Click Undo Slash Redo."* If Dragon NaturallySpeaking does not respond, try saying only the words before the special character. For example, say *"Click Undo."*

TIP *To open the Start menu, say "Click Start."*

To close a menu:

Say *"Cancel"* or press the ESC key.

Selecting buttons, tabs, and options

When Dragon NaturallySpeaking is running, you can select any button, check box, text box, or other dialog box option you see by saying its name. If that doesn't work, say *"Click"* and then its name.

For example, to select a check box labeled "Toolbar," say *"Toolbar"* or *"Click Toolbar."* To clear the check box (unselect it), say its name again.

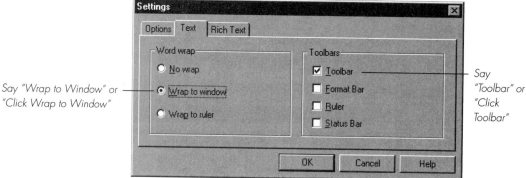

Say "Wrap to Window" or "Click Wrap to Window"

Say "Toolbar" or "Click Toolbar"

You can select tabs by saying the name of the tab, alone or preceded by *"Click."* In the dialog box pictured, you could say *"Options"* or *"Click Options"* to select the Options tab. You can also move between tabs by saying *"Go to Next Tab"* and *"Go to Previous Tab."*

NOTE *In some programs, you may not be able to select dialog box items by saying their names. If this happens, try selecting the items by saying "Tab Key."*

Selecting icons on the desktop

You can use voice commands to select icons on the Windows desktop.

To select an icon on the desktop:

1 Switch to the Windows desktop. (You can't do this by voice.) Say *"Mouse Click"* to make the desktop active.

2 Say the name of the icon (for example, *My Computer*). Dragon NaturallySpeaking types the icon name and Windows selects it.

3 To select another icon, say *"Move"* and then the direction (up, down, left, right) and number of icons (up to 20).

For example, say *"Move Right 1," "Move Down 2,"* or *"Move Up 3."*

Say *"My Computer"* to select My Computer

Say *"Move Right 1"* to select My Briefcase

Say *"Move Down 2"* to select Recycle Bin

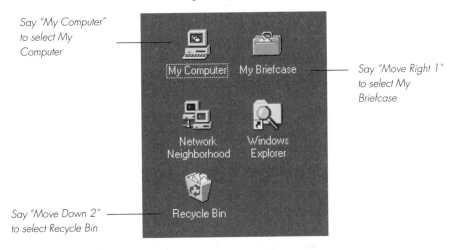

After you select an icon, you can click it by voice. Just say *"Mouse Click," "Mouse Double-Click," "Mouse Left-Click,"* or *"Mouse Right-Click."*

You can also use voice commands to drag the selected object. See "Marking and dragging objects" on page 117.

Resizing and closing windows

To resize and close windows, say *"Click"* and then a window command, such as *"Maximize."* These commands appear on the window's Control menu, but you don't need to open this menu to say them.

> **NOTE** *"Click" is NOT optional for the following Control menu commands.*

To maximize a window:

1 Activate the window you want to maximize.

2 Say *"Click Maximize."*

To minimize a window:

1 Activate the window you want to minimize.

2 Say *"Click Minimize."*

To restore a window to its previous size:

1 Activate the window you want to resize.

2 Say *"Click Restore."*

To close a window:

1 Activate the window you want to close.

2 Say *"Click Close."*

> **NOTE** *If you have trouble getting Dragon NaturallySpeaking to recognize any of the window commands, you can open the Control menu by saying "Click Control Menu" and then say them.*

Scrolling in windows and list boxes

You can scroll vertically in a window (for example, an online Help window) or list box by saying *"Move Down"* and *"Move Up"* and then a number of scroll bar arrow clicks (up to 20). For example, say *"Move Down 4"* or *"Move Up 10."*

You can scroll horizontally by saying *"Move Left"* and *"Move Right"* and then a number of scroll bar arrow clicks (up to 20). For example, say *"Move Left 10"* or *"Move Right 5."*

Pressing keyboard keys

With Dragon NaturallySpeaking, you can "press" any key on your keyboard by voice. You can press letters, numbers, modifier keys (SHIFT, CTRL, and ALT), and so on.

TIP *Dragon NaturallySpeaking version 5 now offers this feature in all editions.*

For example, you can say *"Press a"* and Dragon NaturallySpeaking will type the letter "a" in your document. Or, you can say *"Press Control S"* to press CTRL+S (the keyboard shortcut for saving a document).

TIP *You can say "Press Key" or "Type" instead of "Press."*

You can press keyboard keys when you want to:

- Enter complex text, such as alphanumeric strings (for example, "FD-6389").
- Use keyboard shortcuts without touching the keyboard.

NOTE *"Scratch That" will not erase keystrokes dictated with the Press Key commands. You must select the text and delete it by voice or mouse.*

Pressing letters

You can press any letter on your keyboard by saying *"Press"* and then the letter. When you're pressing letters, you must say *"Press"* before each one. For example, to enter "txt," say *"Press t," "Press x," "Press t."* pausing between letters.

For similar-sounding letters (such as *b, d,* and *v*), you can say *"Press b as in Bill," "Press d as in David,"* and so on (you can also say *"Press b for Bill," "Press d for David,"* and so on) as you would if you were spelling something over the phone. See the complete list below.

TIP *You can use any word in the International Communications Alphabet (page 178) to "spell" the letter keys, for example, Albert/Alice/alpha.*

SAY	THEN *(one)*
Press	(you can also say "for" instead of "as in")
	a
	b
	(any letter a–z)
	a as in Albert/Alice/alpha
	b as in Bill/Buffalo/bravo
	c as in Cathy/Carl/Charlie
	d as in David/daughter/delta
	e as in Edgar/enter/echo
	f as in Frank/fancy/foxtrot
	g as in George/golf/gopher
	h as in Henry/hotel/helmet
	i as in Iris/Ireland/India
	j as in John/justice/Juliet
	k as in Karen/kitchen/kilo
	l as in Larry/lemon/lima
	m as in Mickey/Mike/magic
	n as in Nancy/November/nobody
	o as in Oscar/Otto/over
	p as in Paul/papa/people
	q as in Quentin/Quebec/question
	r as in Robert/Rachel/Romeo
	s as in Sam/Singapore/sierra
	t as in Terry/Tyler/teflon/tango
	u as in Ursula/unit/usual
	v as in Victor/Valerie/visit
	w as in Wendy/whiskey/wake
	x as in Xavier/Xerxes/x-ray
	y as in Yolanda/Yvonne/yankee
	z as in Zachary/zookeeper/zulu

Capitalizing a letter

You can capitalize a letter by saying *"Press Cap"* and then the letter.

For example, to enter "28K" say *"twenty eight"* and then *"Press Cap K"* (or *"Press Cap K for Karen"*).

Pressing numbers

You can press numbers (0 to 9) by saying *"Press"* and then the number. For example, say *"Press 8."*

Pressing key combinations

When you're pressing keys, you can press any combination of the modifier keys (SHIFT, CTRL, and ALT) at the same time as another key, such as a letter. For example, you can say:

■ *"Press Control Z"* (undo)

■ *"Press Alt F"* (opens File menu)

■ *"Press Shift Tab"* (moves backward through dialog box options)

> **NOTE** Dragon NaturallySpeaking ignores the command "Press Control Alt Delete" (the keyboard shortcut for restarting a computer).

Pressing function and numeric keypad keys

To press a function key (F1 to F12), say *"Press Function"* and then the name of the key. For example, say *"Press Function 1"* to bring up the online Help.

To press numeric keypad keys, say *"Press Keypad"* and then the name of the key. For example, you can say *"Press Keypad minus"* to press the keyboard shortcut for correction. See the complete list below:

SAY	THEN (one)
Press	Keypad 1
	Keypad 9 *(you can say any number 0 to 9)*
	All Dialects: Keypad point (.)
	US/Canada: Keypad period (.)
	Other Dialects: Keypad full stop (.)
	Keypad slash (/)
	Keypad asterisk (*)

SAY	THEN *(one)*
	Keypad minus (-) *(opens the Correction dialog box or Quick Correct list, depending on your Correction Options setting)*
	Keypad plus (+) *(turns the microphone on or off)*
	Keypad star (*) *(opens the NaturallySpeaking menu on the DragonBar)*
	Keypad Enter

NOTE *Num Lock must be on for the "Press Keypad" commands to work. You can say "Press Num Lock" to turn Num Lock on.*

Pressing other keys

Here's a list of other keys you can press by voice:

SAY	THEN *(one)*
Press	Up arrow
	Down arrow
	Right arrow
	Left arrow
	Home key
	End key
	Page Up
	Page Down
	Insert key
	Delete key
	Control key
	Shift key
	Alt key
	Print Screen
	Scroll Lock
	Pause key
	Num Lock
	Caps Lock

Moving the mouse pointer and clicking the mouse

Dragon NaturallySpeaking provides hands-free mouse control with MouseGrid™ and the mouse pointer voice commands. You can use these features to position the pointer anywhere on the screen, click the mouse buttons, and drag objects—all by voice.

Moving the mouse pointer with MouseGrid

You can position the mouse pointer anywhere on the screen by using MouseGrid. You can move the pointer relative to the full screen or the active window.

To use MouseGrid:

1 Say *"MouseGrid"* to place the MouseGrid over the full screen (as in this example) or *"MouseGrid Window"* to place it over the active window.

Say "MouseGrid" to place a grid over the full screen

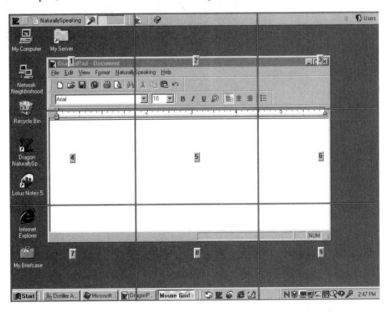

2 Say a grid number from 1 to 9 to position the pointer in that numbered area. In this example, to position the pointer over My Briefcase, say "7." A smaller MouseGrid will appear in the chosen grid square.

Say "7" to place a smaller MouseGrid over grid square number 7.

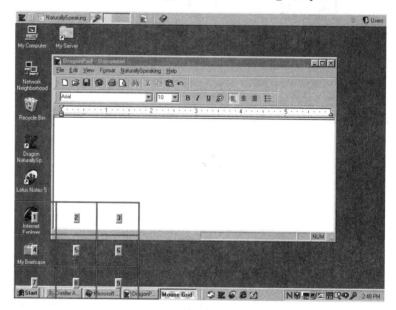

3 To position it again, say another grid number. In this example, say "*4*" to place the pointer directly over the My Briefcase icon.

4 When the pointer is over an icon or other object, you can use voice commands to click the mouse or mark and drag the object. See the following sections for instructions.

TIP *You can undo the last MouseGrid action by saying "Undo That."*

To close MouseGrid, say *"Cancel."*

Moving the pointer with the "Mouse" command

You can move the mouse pointer up, down, left, or right a short distance (a few millimeters) by using the mouse pointer commands.

You can combine moving the mouse pointer and clicking the mouse in a single voice command. For example, you can say *"Mouse Up 3 Click"* or *"Mouse Right 2 Double-Click."*

To move the pointer:

1   Say *"Mouse"* followed by the direction and number of times to move it (up to 10). For example, say *"Mouse Up 5"* or *"Mouse Left 10."*

2   When the pointer is over an icon or other object, you can use voice commands to click the mouse or mark and drag the object.

> **NOTE** *It's not possible to start the mouse moving without specifying a number of units. For example, saying just "Mouse Down" doesn't work.*

Clicking the mouse

You can click, double-click, left-click, and right-click the mouse button by voice.

To click the mouse:

1   Position the mouse pointer over the object you want to select (for example, say *"MouseGrid 9 1"* or *"Mouse 2"*).

2   Say *"Mouse Click," "Mouse Double-Click," "Mouse Left-Click,"* or *"Mouse Right-Click."*

When an object is selected, you can mark and drag the object (as described in the next section).

Marking and dragging objects

You can mark an object and drag it to a different location by voice.

To mark and drag an object:

1   Position the mouse over the icon or object you want to drag, and then say *"Mark"* (for example, say *"MouseGrid 9 1 Mark"*).

2   Move the mouse pointer to where you want to drag the object, and then say *"Drag"* (for example, say *"MouseGrid 6 3 Drag"*).

> **TIP** *Instead of "Drag," you can also say "Control-Drag" and "Shift-Drag" to drag while holding down the CTRL or SHIFT key.*

CHAPTER 7

Working With E-Mail and the Web

Imagine answering your e-mail as easily as you answer the telephone: by voice. Dragon NaturallySpeaking version 5 now works with most popular e-mail applications and with Lotus Notes (Professional and higher editions). If you use Internet Explorer® to browse the Web, you can also use Dragon NaturallySpeaking to follow links and go to your favorite sites.

This chapter describes how to:

- Work with popular e-mail applications
- Work with Internet Explorer 4 or 5

You can start and control most programs by voice. (If voice commands don't work in a particular program, that program is probably not designed for "hands-free" use.)

Working with E-mail

Now you can dictate outgoing e-mail messages and have your computer read incoming messages to you. Dragon NaturallySpeaking works with these and other popular e-mail applications:

- America OnLine® 4.0 or 5.0
- QUALCOMM® Eudora® Pro 4.3
- Lotus Notes 5.0 (Professional and higher editions; see online Help)
- Microsoft Outlook® 97, 98, or 2000
- Microsoft Outlook Express 5
- Netscape® Messenger® in Netscape Communicator® 4.73

When Dragon NaturallySpeaking and your e-mail application are running, you can use voice commands to:

- Check for new mail
- Open and close incoming mail
- Compose mail by dictating
- Transfer dictation into your e-mail
- Forward and reply to mail
- Send and print mail messages
- Delete mail messages

Checking for new mail

You must be connected to the Internet to check your e-mail. Your e-mail program must also be open. For more information on starting programs and controlling your computer by voice, see Chapter 6, "Working With Your Desktop and Windows."

To check for new mail, say *"Check For New Mail"* or *"Check For E-Mail."* This command checks your Inbox for new messages.

TIP *You can say "Mail," "Message," "Memo," or "E-Mail" interchangeably in any of the e-mail commands.*

Opening and closing mail

To open a mail message, select it and say *"Open Mail."* Once a message is selected, you can also say *"Open That."* To close an open message, say *"Close Mail."*

TIP *You can move to the message and select it by "pressing" function and arrow keys by voice (see "Pressing keyboard keys," page 111) or using the Move commands (see page 89).*

Composing mail

To compose a new message, say *"New Mail"* or *"New Message."* Once the new blank message appears, you can navigate to any field by voice and start dictating.

To navigate e-mail fields:

SAY	THEN (one)
Go to	To Field
Move to	CC Field
	BCC Field
	Body Field
	First Field
	Last Field

Here's an example of how to dictate a simple e-mail message.

To dictate an e-mail message:

1 Say *"New Mail."* The new message opens on your screen.

2 Say *"Go to To Field."* Pause (to make sure you are in the correct field), then dictate the recipient's e-mail address, for example *"harriet at dragonsystems dot com."* If you are entering more than one address, separate each one by saying *"comma."*

3 (optional) Say *"Go to CC Field"* or *"Go to BCC Field,"* pause, and dictate the addresses of the people who should receive copies, or blind copies, of your message.

> **TIP** *In many e-mail programs, you can also say just "Subject" or "BCC" to move to the field by that name.*

4 Say *"Go to Subject Field,"* pause, and dictate the subject of your message, for example *"Planning A Trip To See You."*

5 Say *"Go to Body Field,"* pause, and begin dictating the body of your message.

See the online Tutorial and your *Quick Start* guide for more detailed information on dictating and formatting e-mail.

Transferring dictation into your e-mail

If you have dictated text into another program such as the DragonPad, or have transcribed text from a mobile recorder, you can transfer it into an e-mail message.

To transfer dictation from the DragonPad into e-mail:

1 Say "*Switch to DragonPad.*" Dictate your message, or open a previously transcribed document.

2 Say "*Copy All to Clipboard.*" The entire document is selected and transferred to the clipboard.

3 Say "*Switch To*" followed by the name of your e-mail program. For example, say "*Switch to Eudora.*"

4 Say "*Go to Body Field*" to move the insertion point to the message body.

5 Say "*Paste That*" to transfer your text into your e-mail message.

Sending and printing mail

Once your message is ready to send, you can simply say "*Send Mail*" to send your e-mail on its way. To print a message, say "*Print Mail*" and the message will be sent to your printer.

Forwarding and replying to mail

To forward a message selected in your Inbox, simply say "*Forward Mail*," then dictate the recipient's address in the To Field of the new message.

Select a message and say "*Reply to Mail*" to create a new message addressed to the sender. To reply to everyone on the mailing list, say "*Reply To All.*" Then move to the Body Field and dictate your reply.

Deleting mail

You can delete the currently selected message by saying "*Delete Mail.*" This command will work on all selected messages, so make sure you have selected only those you want to delete.

NOTE *You cannot use e-mail commands when editing mail in the Word editor started by Outlook. In Outlook 2000, you select the Word editor on the Mail Format tab of the Options dialog box, which you open using the the Options command on the Tools menu. Outlook uses the Word editor for messages if you select Use Microsoft Word to edit email messages and you set the message format to HTML or plain text. Also, make sure the option to Allow Natural Language Commands in Microsoft Word (on the Startup/ Shutdown tab of the Options dialog box) is not selected.*

Working with Internet Explorer

You can use Dragon NaturallySpeaking to control Internet Explorer and browse the Web by voice. To use this feature, you must have Internet Explorer version 4.0 or later installed.

When Dragon NaturallySpeaking and Internet Explorer are running, you can use voice commands to:

- Go to any Web page on the Favorites menu
- Enter a Web address (URL) in the Address bar
- Go back to the previous Web page or forward to the next
- Click links, words, buttons, and images
- Scroll in a Web page
- Select check boxes and other options
- Enter text in a text box (such as a Search box)

Follow these steps whenever you want to use Dragon NaturallySpeaking with Internet Explorer.

To use Internet Explorer by voice:

1 Start Dragon NaturallySpeaking. If Internet Explorer is running, close it first.

> **NOTE** *Always start Dragon NaturallySpeaking before you start Internet Explorer.*

2 Start Internet Explorer. You can say *"Start Internet Explorer."*

> **NOTE** *If you cannot control Internet Explorer 4.0 by voice, it may mean that an Internet Explorer option required for voice control is not selected. From the Internet Explorer View menu, select Internet Options, and then click the Advanced tab. Make sure the "Browse in a new process" box is checked.*

Going to favorite Web pages

You can use voice commands to go to any Web site saved in your list of Favorites. You can also use voice commands to add a Web page to the Favorites menu.

To go to a Favorites page:

Say *"Go to Favorite"* and then the name of the favorite page exactly as it appears in the Favorites menu.

For example, say *"Go to Favorite Yahoo"* or *"Go to Favorite Dragon Systems."* You cannot use voice commands to go to the Channels folder.

> **TIP** *If Dragon NaturallySpeaking misunderstands your command and opens the wrong page, you can return to where you were by saying "Go Back."*

To add a page to the Favorites menu:

1 Go to the page you want to add to the Favorites menu.

2 Say *"Click Favorites"* to open the Favorites menu.

3 Say *"Add to Favorites"* to open the Add Favorites dialog box.

4 Type a name for the page (you cannot dictate text into this box). Select a short name, so it will be easy to open the page by voice.

5 Save the page anywhere on the Favorites menu.

6 Click or say *"OK"* to close the Add Favorites dialog box.

Entering a Web address in the Address bar

You can dictate Web addresses (URLs) in the Internet Explorer Address bar.

To enter a Web address:

1 Say *"Go to Address"* to move to the Address bar.

Address bar —————————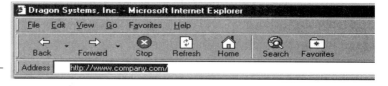

2 Dictate the Web address (for example, say *"w w w dot dragon systems dot com"*). Most URLs are not case-sensitive, but you may need to say *"Cap"* if your web address contains capital letters.

For more information about dictating Web addresses, see "Dictating e-mail and Web addresses" on page 72.

3 Say *"Go There"* to open the page (same as pressing the ENTER key).

TIP *You can also say "Click Go" instead of "Go There."*

Going back to the previous Web page or forward to the next

You can go back to the previous Web page by saying *"Go Back"* (same as clicking the Back button on the Internet Explorer toolbar).

To go forward to the next Web page, say *"Go Forward"* (same as clicking the Forward button on the Internet Explorer toolbar).

Here's a list of the voice commands you can use to control the Internet Explorer toolbar:

SAY	TO
Go To Address	Move the insertion point to the Address box.
Click Go *or* Go There	Go to the Web address in the Address box.
Go To Favorite *Dragon Systems*	Load a page that is on your Favorites list, in this example, *Dragon Systems*.
Go Back	Go back to the previous Web page (same as clicking the Back button).
Go Forward	Go forward to the previous Web page (same as clicking the Forward button).
Stop Loading	Stop a Web page from loading (same as clicking the Stop button).
Refresh *or* Reload	Refresh the current Web page (same as clicking the Refresh button).
Go Home	Go to your home page (same as clicking the Home button).

Entering text in a text box

When Dragon NaturallySpeaking is running, you can dictate text into text boxes on a Web page (for example, into Search boxes).

To enter text in a text box:

1 Say *"Type Text"* to move to the first text box on the page.

> **TIP** You can also say "Edit Box" or "Text Field" instead of "Type Text."

2 If the page has more than one text box, they will be numbered like this 📭 . (See the following procedures for examples.) Choose the number you want, or move to the next or previous text box by saying *"Next"* or *"Previous."*

3 When the insertion point is in a text box, you can dictate text.

In text boxes, you can also correct recognition mistakes and use Select-and-Say for revisions, just as you do when you're dictating into a document.

Clicking links, words, buttons, and images

You can click the text links and buttons on a Web page simply by saying the link (for example, the underlined words) or button name.

If the text link or button name is long, you don't need to say all of it. Just say enough to distinguish it from other links on the page.

To click a text link:

1 Say the text link (must be visible on the screen). For example, to click Stock Quotes on the page pictured below, say *"Stock Quotes."*

2 An arrow ⬆ appears briefly to indicate which link was selected, and then the page opens.

> **TIP** You can also say "Click" and then the link text. For example, you could say "Click News and events." Sometimes saying "Click" first, then pausing, is more reliable than just saying the link text alone.

3 If more than one link matches what you said (for example, if there are two links on the page named "Auctions"), Dragon NaturallySpeaking numbers all the links on the page like this 📭 .

4 If this is not the link you want, you can move to the next or previous matching link by saying another number, or by saying *"Next"* or *"Previous."*

Say *"Stock Quotes"* to open this unique link.

Say *"Choose 1"* to move to the first *"Auctions."*

Say *"Choose 2"* or *"Next"* to move to the second *"Auctions."*

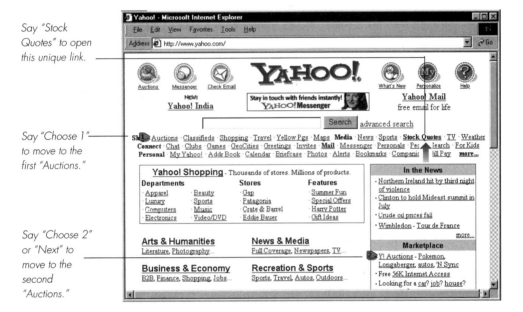

NOTE *On secure Web pages this feature is disabled. You cannot select links on secure pages by voice.*

To click an image:

1 When you say *"Image"* (or *"Click Image"*), Dragon NaturallySpeaking numbers all the images on the page like this ➊.

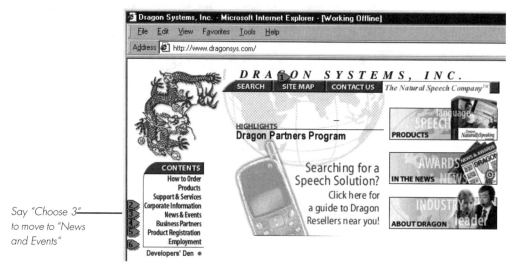

Say *"Choose 3"* to move to *"News and Events"*

2 Move to the image you want by saying, for example, *"Choose 3."*

3 If this is not the image you want, you can choose another number or move to the next or previous one by saying *"Next"* or *"Previous."*

> **TIP** *If Dragon NaturallySpeaking misunderstands your command and opens the wrong page, you can return to where you were by saying "Go Back."*

To click a button:

Say the button name. For example, to click the button pictured below, say *"Search."*

You can also say *"Click"* and then the button name. For example, you could say *"Click Search"* (or *"Click Search Button"*).

To unselect the button, you must select a different one.

To click a check box, list box, or radio (option) button:

1 Say "*Check Box*," "*List Box*," or "*Radio Button*" to number the buttons like this 🔷 . Then choose the number you want as in the previous procedure.

Here is a table of commands you can use for clicking links, images, check boxes, and buttons.

SAY	TO
Type Text *or* Edit Box	Go to the first place on a Web page where you can enter text.
Click Check Box *or* Check Box	Number all check boxes on the page, and go to the first one.
Click Image *or* Image	Number all images with links on the page, and go to the first one.
Choose 2	Select the image, option, button, and so on from the numbered list of choices. You can say any number that appears in the list.
Click Radio Button/ Radio Button	Number all option (radio) buttons on the page, and go to the first one.
Click List Box *or* List Box	Number all boxes with a list of choices (drop-down lists) on the page, and go to the first one.
Show Choices	Open a list of choices.
Hide Choices	Close a list of choices.
Choose *Thursday or Thursday*	Choose an entry from a list of choices, in this example, *Thursday*.

Scrolling in a Web page

When Dragon NaturallySpeaking is running, you can scroll in a Web page by voice. You can use voice commands to go to the top or bottom of a page, or to move up or down a screen or line at a time.

You can also start automatic scrolling by saying "*Start Scrolling Down*" or "*Start Scrolling Up.*" Automatic scrolling is convenient when you want to read a Web page without using the mouse or keyboard. See the complete list of commands below:

SAY	TO
Go to Bottom	Scroll to the end of the Web page.
Go to Top	Scroll to the beginning of the Web page.
Page Down	Scroll down one screen (same as pressing the Page Down key).
Page Up	Scroll up one screen (same as pressing the Page Up key).
Line Down	Scroll down one line (same as clicking the down arrow in the scroll bar once).
Line Up	Scroll up one line (same as clicking the up arrow in the scroll bar once).
Start Scrolling Down	Start automatic scrolling toward the end of the page.
Start Scrolling Up	Start automatic scrolling toward the beginning of the page.
Speed Up	Increase scrolling speed. (Say it again to speed up more.)
Slow Down	Decrease scrolling speed. (Say it again to slow down more.)
Stop Scrolling	Stop automatic scrolling.

While a Web page is scrolling, you can click the text links and buttons you see by voice if the page is moving slowly enough.

CHAPTER 8

Managing Users

M ore than one person can use Dragon NaturallySpeaking on the same computer. You can even dictate in different languages or dialects (Preferred and higher editions).

Each person who wants to use the program needs to create a new set of user speech files and train Dragon NaturallySpeaking to understand his or her voice. A single person might want to have more than one set of user speech files (called a *user*) if, for example, you dictate into a mobile recorder or in more than one language.

What are user speech files?

Your user speech files contain all the information that Dragon NaturallySpeaking gathers about you: your pronunciation, your vocabulary, how often you use certain words, and your preferences (whether you want one or two spaces after a period or a full stop, for example).

The Users menu on the right side of the DragonBar lists all available users.

When you share Dragon NaturallySpeaking with others, you're prompted to choose your user name from a list whenever you start the program. This lets Dragon NaturallySpeaking know which user speech files to load. If the program is already running, make sure your own user is open before you start dictating.

This chapter explains how to set up Dragon NaturallySpeaking so that more than one person can use it, and describes how to open, rename, delete, back up, and restore users.

Creating a new user

When someone new wants to use Dragon NaturallySpeaking, that person needs to follow the steps described in this section to create a new user.

To create a new user:

1 On the far right of the DragonBar, click Users and then click Manage Users.

Or, from the NaturallySpeaking menu, point to Advanced, and then click Manage Users.

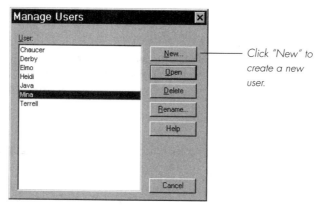

Click "New" to create a new user.

▲ *The Manage Users dialog box lists the names of all users.*

2 In the Manage Users dialog box, click New.

3 Follow the steps in the New User Wizard.

> **TIP** *As you complete the steps in the New User Wizard, you can find step-by-step instructions on creating a user in your Quick Start guide.*

Opening a user

When someone else has been using Dragon NaturallySpeaking, you need to open your own user before you start using the program. Or, if you have more than one user of your own (for example, you have a separate user for your portable recorder), always remember to switch to the appropriate user before you start.

To open a user:

1   On the far right of the DragonBar, select Users and then click Manage Users.

2   Select a user and click Open.

This loads your speech files. These files include information about your pronunciation that Dragon NaturallySpeaking needs to recognize your voice.

TIP *You can also open a user from the Manage Users dialog box by clicking Open.*

Renaming a user

You can change the name of a user at any time.

To rename a user:

1   On the far right of the DragonBar, click Users and then click Manage Users. The Manage Users dialog box opens.

2   Select a user and click Rename.

3   Type a new name and click OK.

The name can contain up to 128 characters, including spaces. Special characters are not allowed in user names.

4   To close the Manage Users dialog box, click Cancel.

Deleting a user

If you know you will not need a user that you have created, you can delete it and free up hard-disk space. Removing a user can't be undone, so make sure you don't need it before you remove it.

To delete a user:

1 On the far right of the DragonBar, select Users and then click Manage Users.

2 In the Manage Users dialog box, select the user you want to delete and click Delete.

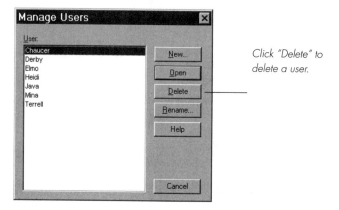

Click "Delete" to delete a user.

3 A dialog box will appear asking if you really want to permanently remove this user. To confirm, click "Yes." To cancel, click "No."

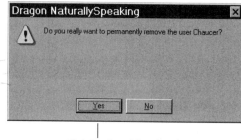

Click "Yes" to delete the user permanently.

If you want to delete the current user, you must close it first by opening a different user.

There must be at least one user on the computer, so if you've got only one, you can't delete it.

NOTE *Always use the Delete button to delete users. Don't remove folders from the \...NaturallySpeaking\Users folder on your hard disk. Using the Delete button is the only way to completely remove all information about a user from your computer.*

Backing up a user

When you make changes to your user (for example, by adding words to the vocabulary), Dragon NaturallySpeaking prompts you to save your user speech files. The program automatically makes a backup copy every fifth time you save your speech files.

You can change the frequency of automatic backups or turn this feature off. On the NaturallySpeaking menu, point to Advanced, click Options, and then click the Miscellaneous tab.

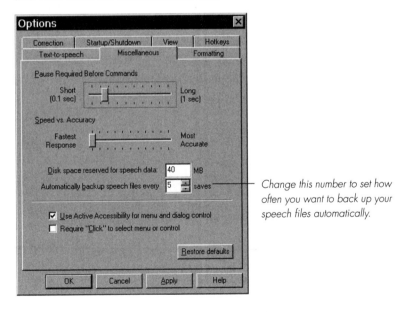

Change this number to set how often you want to back up your speech files automatically.

To back up your current user manually, follow these steps.

NOTE *You can only back up the current user. You cannot back up a user simply by selecting it in the Manage Users dialog box; you must open the user first.*

To back up a user:

1 Open the user you want to back up.

2 From the NaturallySpeaking menu, point to Advanced and click Backup User.

Dragon NaturallySpeaking makes a backup copy in a default location on your computer.

NOTE *It's not possible to create a backup in a different place or on removable media.*

If you made recent changes to your user (for example, added words to the vocabulary), Dragon NaturallySpeaking prompts you to save these changes before it makes the backup.

Restoring a backup copy of a user

If you make unwanted changes to your speech files (for example, you process the wrong documents in Vocabulary Builder), you can restore the last backup copy of your user. Again, you can only restore the current user.

To restore a user:

1 Open the user you want to restore, for example, "Elmo."

2 From the NaturallySpeaking menu, point to Advanced and click Restore User.

Dragon NaturallySpeaking restores the last backup that was made and saves it with a different name, for example, "Elmo - Restored1."

3 Open the restored user to begin working with it. Select it from the Users menu on the DragonBar, or click Manage Users, select the user name, and click Open.

Delete the older version (in this example, the user named "Elmo") and rename the one you just restored.

Multilingual users

Dragon NaturallySpeaking version 5 allows you to create and train users in multiple languages. If you have purchased a product with support for more than one language, you can add additional languages by choosing "Custom Install" during Setup. If you didn't select additional languages during Setup, you will still be able to select them when you create a new user. You will need to insert the CD to install the new language files. See your *Quick Start* guide for more information about installation.

Once you have installed a new language (for example, Spanish), follow the instructions in this chapter to create and train a user in that language. Once that user is open, you will see the Dragon NaturallySpeaking menus and dialog boxes switch to the new language (in this example, Spanish), and all commands and dictation will work in the language of that user.

To change between languages, open a user in the language you want to switch to (for example, English). After that user loads, the menus and commands will be restored to that language (in this example, English), and you can resume dictating in that language.

TIP *If two English speakers share a computer but dictate in different dialects (for example, US English and UK English), just create a user for each one and make sure to switch your Windows Regional Settings accordingly. You may need to do a Custom Install to add the appropriate dialect (language) files; follow the instructions on the screen.*

Tips for multilingual users

- When you switch between users with different languages, only the DragonBar and DragonPad change the language of their menus and dialog boxes. The language of other programs you use (for example, Microsoft Word, WordPerfect, and Lotus Notes) will not change. You will still be able to dictate in the new language, but you may find it difficult to navigate through menus using voice commands.

- The Dragon NaturallySpeaking Tutorial will be available only for the first language you installed. In order to run the Tutorial in languages you add later, you must install the Tutorial from the CD for each additional language.

■ In Lotus Notes, you will only be able to use e-mail commands if the language of the Lotus Notes mail file matches the language of your user.

■ If you switch users to dictate text in multiple languages in the same document, you will be able to correct and change text in both languages. Multilingual correction works best with the mouse.

■ When you select text in a language different from your current user, the Quick Correct list and Correction dialog box will display choices in the language of the text you select. Whatever you choose from the list will be typed into your document in the correct language, but Dragon NaturallySpeaking will not adapt your current user's speech files with changes you make in the other language.

■ If you have recognition problems when revising text transcribed in a different language, switch back to the user whose language matches the dictated text.

■ To protect your recognition accuracy, run Vocabulary Builder only on documents in the language of your current user. If you combine languages in one document, or add many foreign language words to a user's vocabulary (especially without training their pronunciation), Dragon NaturallySpeaking could have problems recognizing words in the user's original language, leading to recognition mistakes.

CHAPTER 9

Creating Your Own Dragon NaturallySpeaking Commands

With Dragon NaturallySpeaking Professional and higher editions, you can expand the power of the program by creating your own voice commands for tasks you do frequently.

Commands can insert multiple lines of text into the current document, send keystrokes to the current program, or run complex scripts. For example, you could create commands to do the following:

- Insert your mailing address when you say *"Type My Address."*

- Automatically set margins and change font styles when you say *"Format My Letter."*

- Open a new e-mail message and address it to one of a list of people when you say *"Send Mail to Pat," "Send Mail to Steve,"* and so on.

This chapter provides general information about commands, explains how to create and edit your own commands (including a step-by-step example of creating a voice command to insert a closing remark into a Microsoft Word document), discusses how to import and export command files, and offers troubleshooting tips for custom commands.

This chapter does not cover use of the Dragon NaturallySpeaking scripting language for creating complex commands. See the *Dragon NaturallySpeaking: Creating Voice Commands* guide or the online Help for more information.

About voice commands

You can create your own voice commands only with Dragon NaturallySpeaking Professional and higher editions.

In Chapter 4, "Dictating Names, Numbers & Punctuation," you learned how to create *dictation shortcuts* for entering words or blocks of text that you use frequently. Commands are similar to dictation shortcuts, but are much more powerful.

You can use custom commands to "press" any sequence of keys on the keyboard (including special characters), or run complex scripts (a series of computer instructions).

Commands are stored in special data files (usually ending in the extension .dvc, for Dragon voice commands). You don't work directly with these command files. Instead, you create your own commands by using the New Command Wizard described in the next section.

Commands can be active everywhere (global commands) or only in certain programs or windows (application-specific commands). The next section describes how to specify where a command is active.

Creating and editing voice commands

When you want to create a new voice command, you use the New Command Wizard. (To edit a command with the Edit Command Wizard, see page 148.)

To create a new command:

From the NaturallySpeaking menu, point to Custom Commands and click Create. The New Command Wizard guides you through the steps.

To create the new command, you'll need to:

- Specify where the command will be active
- Create a file to store the command

- Name the command
- Specify what the command will do

After creating a command, if you need to make changes to it (for example, change its name or what it does), you can edit it by using the Edit Command Wizard. See "Editing a command" on page 148 for more information.

Specifying where a command will be active

When creating a new command, the first step is to decide whether you want the command to be active in all programs (global command) or only in a specific program (application-specific command).

If the command would be useful in different programs, you should make it global. For example, if you're creating a command for printing a document, make it global so that you can use it in your word processor, e-mail program, and so on.

If the command applies to only one program, you should make it application-specific. For example, if you're creating a command for automatically formatting a Corel WordPerfect document, make it application-specific to Corel WordPerfect.

The New Command Wizard prompts you to select the specific program. In order to see the program listed in the New Command Wizard, you will need to start the program if it is not already running.

Creating a command file

After specifying where the command will be active, the next step is to name the file where the command will be stored.

You should usually avoid creating new commands in the command files that came with Dragon NaturallySpeaking. These are the ones that do *not* have a star * next to them in the list of available command files.

Putting custom commands in their own command files not only makes it easier to distinguish your own commands from the standard built-in commands, but also makes upgrading easier in the future. Dragon NaturallySpeaking cannot upgrade command files that you have modified.

Application-specific commands

If the command is application-specific, you will then be asked to select the title of the target window or dialog box for the command. The command will work only in the specified window or dialog box of the program you select. For example, you could specify that a command *"Resize Table"* should work only when that program's Table dialog box is open.

You will usually want to store application-specific commands in a separate file for each program, though you might want to make an exception if you have several programs that work closely together. One advantage to using separate files is that Dragon NaturallySpeaking only loads the command files as needed, so you will save time and memory by loading only the commands you will be using.

Naming a command

After storing the command in a file, the next step is to give the command a name. The command name is the phrase you say to execute the command, for example, *"Type My Address."*

Here are some guidelines for naming commands:

- Choose a short phrase that you're unlikely to need in your writing. Phrases of two to five words are best, because they're easier for Dragon NaturallySpeaking to recognize.
- Don't start a command with a common word, such as "the" or "a."
- Avoid using punctuation. If a command name contains punctuation, you must say it to use the command.
- (optional) For consistency with other Dragon NaturallySpeaking commands, capitalize each word in the command name.

Specifying what a command will do

After naming the command, the next step is to specify what the command will do. The command can either type text and "press" keys (for example, press CTRL+P to open the Print dialog box) or run a script.

After you select the type of command action, the New Command Wizard prompts you to enter the text and keystrokes or write the script. For information about writing scripts, see the online Help or consult your *Dragon NaturallySpeaking: Creating Voice Commands* guide.

Example: Creating a command "Type Closing Remark"

Suppose you want to create a command named "Type Closing Remark" that moves to the bottom of your Microsoft Word document and types "Dictated with Dragon NaturallySpeaking."

On the NaturallySpeaking menu, point to Custom Commands and then click Create.

Then follow these steps to create the command:

To create "Type Closing Remark":

1 Select the type of command you want to create.

For this example, select Application-specific.

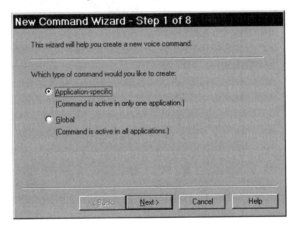

To continue, click Next.

2 Select the program in which you want the command to be active.

> **TIP** *If you don't see the program in the New Command Wizard window, that means it's not already active, so you should start the program and then return to the New Command Wizard.*

For this example, select Microsoft Word.

You can drag the crosshair pointer to a program window to select it.

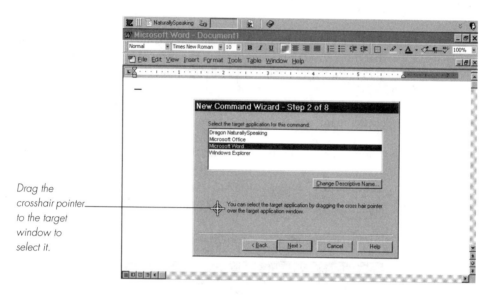

Drag the crosshair pointer to the target window to select it.

To continue, click Next.

3 Select the file where you want the command to be active, or enter a new file name.

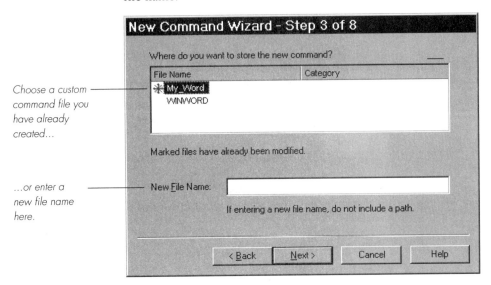

Choose a custom command file you have already created...

...or enter a new file name here.

By default, the computer chooses the command file associated with the program for which you create the command (in this example, WINWORD). For global commands, the default file is the global.dvc file. You should not accept this choice unless you want to modify the command file that came with Dragon NaturallySpeaking.

It is better to enter a unique file name in this step, especially if you want to share this command with other users. Command files you've already modified appear in the list with a star ✳.

To continue, click Next.

4 Select the specific window or dialog box in which you want the command to be active.

Your command will work whenever the window title you specify in this step matches the window title of the active window or dialog box.

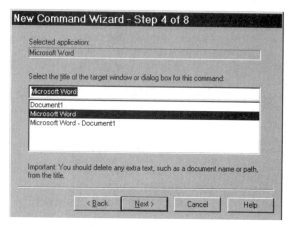

To continue, click Next.

5 Enter the command name.

For this example, enter "Type Closing Remark."

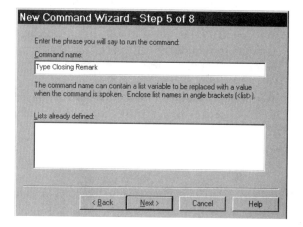

To continue, click Next.

6 Select the type of command action.

For this example, select Type text or keystrokes.

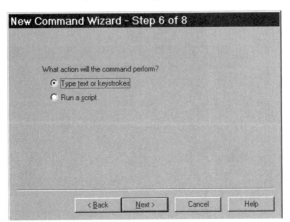

To continue, click Next.

7 In the Keystrokes box, type the text and keystrokes you want the command to type or send.

For this example, type the text string "{Ctrl+End}," then "{Ctrl+b},"
followed by the text "Dictated with Dragon NaturallySpeaking" and
"{Ctrl+b}" again.

This instructs the program to send the keystrokes CTRL+END (the
keyboard shortcut for moving to the end of the page), turn Bold
formatting on (by typing CTRL+b), type your closing remark, and apply
the Bold formatting to the entire phrase.

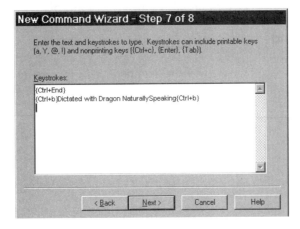

To continue, click Next.

8 Check your selections.

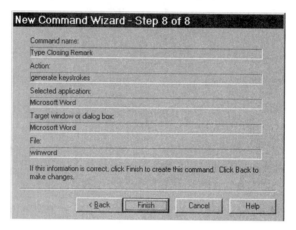

To close the wizard and create the command, click Finish. If you need to make changes, click Back.

9 Try your new command.

The command is application-specific, so you must first switch to the window where it's active (in this example, Microsoft Word).

Say *"Type Closing Remark."* Remember to pause briefly before saying the command, but not in the middle of the command phrase.

If you have trouble getting your command to work, see the online Help.

Editing a command

You can use the Edit Command wizard to rename and delete commands, edit command actions, and change the target window for application-specific commands. You can edit not only commands you create but also most standard Dragon NaturallySpeaking commands.

Edit standard commands with caution

If you modify standard Dragon NaturallySpeaking commands, do so cautiously; these commands were selected to be easily distinguished from dictation words.

You cannot modify correction commands, such as "Scratch That" and "Correct That," or dictation commands, such as "New Paragraph" and "All Caps On."

To edit a command:

1 From the NaturallySpeaking menu, point to Custom Commands, and then click Edit.

2 When the Edit Command wizard appears, follow the instructions in the wizard. If you need additional instructions, click the wizard Help button.

3 When you have finished editing the command, click Finish in the Edit Command wizard.

You may want to make a backup copy of your custom command files (.dvc files) in your Users folder before modifying or deleting commands.

NOTE *If you are using an Enterprise (network) edition of Dragon NaturallySpeaking, contact your Dragon NaturallySpeaking administrator to make backup copies of your custom command files found in your user's current directory on the network.*

Renaming a command

You can use the Edit Command wizard to rename any custom command you have created for the current user. Follow the procedure in the previous section on how to edit a command.

TIP *Instead of renaming a command, you can create a new command that performs the same action but has a different name. For example, you could create a command named "Erase That" that performs the same action as "Scratch That."*

Importing and deleting command files

Dragon NaturallySpeaking can only import and export command files, not individual commands. If you want to share a groups of commands with other people, it makes sense to put all the commands you might be sharing together in a single file. You may also choose to organize groups of commands into separate files according to what the commands do.

Importing command files

The Import Commands dialog box allows you to import custom voice commands created by other Dragon NaturallySpeaking users. After importing a voice command file, you can use all the custom voice commands it contains, in addition to any custom voice commands that were already in your voice command file. You can also edit commands that are contained in the imported file.

To import command files:

1 On the Custom Commands submenu, click Import.

2 Use the Look In box to navigate to the location of the voice command file (for example, Mycommands.dvc) that you want to import.

Voice command files are located in the *users\<UserName>\current* directory, where *<UserName>* is the name of the user who created the voice command.

3 Click Import. The status of the import process and any error messages appear in the Import Status dialog box.

You can also delete command files you have imported.

Deleting command files

Use the following procedure to delete a file containing a set of voice commands that you have imported from another Dragon NaturallySpeaking user.

To delete a command file:

1 On the Custom Commands menu, click Delete.

2 Select the command file you want to delete in the Command File to Delete list.

3 Click Delete.

Deleting a command cannot be undone. You may want to make a backup copy of your custom command files (.dvc files) in your Users folder before modifying or deleting command files.

NOTE *If you are using an Enterprise (network) edition of Dragon NaturallySpeaking, contact your Dragon NaturallySpeaking administrator to make backup copies of your custom command files found in your user's current directory on the network.*

Troubleshooting commands

Custom commands may not run properly in every situation. If a command cannot run, it displays an error message.

If a command you have created produces an error or does nothing, use the Edit Command wizard to open the command and check the following information:

- If the command is application-specific, is the correct window or dialog box active when you say the command?
- If so, does the title of the active window match the title specified?
- If the command includes keystrokes, are curly brackets included around keystrokes (for example, {CTRL+b} for bold)? Are the key codes correct?
- If the command name contains punctuation (for example, *"What Time Is It?"*), did you include the punctuation in the command name, as in the example below?

  what time is it question mark
- If the command includes a list, do the list values match what you said?

Using Dragon NaturallySpeaking With a Portable Recorder

If you have Dragon NaturallySpeaking Preferred or a higher edition, you can dictate into a portable recorder and then use Dragon NaturallySpeaking to transcribe your recorded speech.

This appendix describes how you can use Dragon NaturallySpeaking with the Dragon NaturallyMobile™ recorder, the Sony® Memory Stick™ IC Recorder ICD-MS1, the Sony ICD-R100 recorder, or with other recorders that have been certified by Dragon Systems. A current list of certified recorders is available at www.dragonsystems.com.

To prepare Dragon NaturallySpeaking for use with a recorder, follow these steps:

- Install the recorder software (required only for certain recorders)
- Create a user specifically adapted to the sound of your recorded speech

Once you have created a user, follow these steps whenever you want to use your recorder with Dragon NaturallySpeaking:

- Dictate into your recorder
- Transcribe the recorded dictation
- Correct mistakes

Installing recorder software

The Sony Memory Stick IC Recorder ICD-MS1 and the Sony ICD-R100 recorder require additional software to work with Dragon NaturallySpeaking.

■ If you are using the Sony Memory Stick IC Recorder ICD-MS1, you must install the Sony Memory Stick Voice Editor.

■ If you are using the Sony ICD-R100 recorder, you must install the ICD-PCLINK software.

■ If you are using the Dragon NaturallyMobile recorder, you can install the Voice It® Link™ software, which is not required, but can enhance the recorder's usability.

This software is available on your Dragon NaturallySpeaking CD but it is not automatically installed when you install Dragon NaturallySpeaking. To install the recorder software, use the appropriate procedure from among the following:

To install Sony Memory Stick Voice Editor (for the Sony Memory Stick IC recorder ICD-MS1):

1 Put the Dragon NaturallySpeaking CD in the CD-ROM reader of your computer.

2 Using Windows Explorer, go to the MSVE folder of the Dragon NaturallySpeaking CD. The folder is on the top level directory of the Dragon NaturallySpeaking CD.

3 Double-click Setup and follow the instructions of the Setup wizard.

To install ICD-PCLINK (for the Sony ICD-R100 recorder):

1 Put the Dragon NaturallySpeaking CD in the CD-ROM reader of your computer.

2 Using Windows Explorer, go to the PCLINK folder of the Dragon NaturallySpeaking CD. The folder is on the top level directory of the Dragon NaturallySpeaking CD.

3 Double-click Setup and follow the instructions of the Setup wizard.

Use the Voice It Link software to perform functions for your Dragon NaturallyMobile recorder that you can't perform from the Dragon NaturallySpeaking Transcribe dialog box. Note that for normal transcription from the Dragon NaturallyMobile recorder, you don't need to have this software installed.

To install Voice It Link (for the Dragon NaturallyMobile recorder):

1 Put the Dragon NaturallySpeaking CD in the CD-ROM reader of your computer.

2 Using Windows Explorer, go to the VOICEIT folder of the Dragon NaturallySpeaking CD. The folder is on the top level directory of the Dragon NaturallySpeaking CD.

3 Double-click Setup and follow the instructions of the Setup wizard.

Creating a user adapted to your recorded speech

Before you can use Dragon NaturallySpeaking with a portable recorder, you must create a user specifically adapted to the sound of your recorded speech. You do this by running the New User Wizard and selecting one of the recorder options as the dictation source.

NOTE *Steps 1 and 2 assume that you have already created a headset microphone user (see "Creating a new user" on page 132). If you have not previously created a user for Dragon NaturallySpeaking, then the New User Wizard will appear when you first start the program, and you can skip to step 3.*

To create a user:

1 From the NaturallySpeaking menu, point to Advanced, and click Manage Users. You can also click the Users button on the DragonBar, and then click Manage Users.

2 In the Manage Users dialog box, click New.

The New User wizard guides you through the steps of creating a user. As you complete the steps, click Next whenever you are ready to continue.

3 On the Create User screen, enter a unique name for the user. Make sure that the language and vocabulary are correct for your system (see your *Quick Start* guide for details). Then select the appropriate recorder type from the dictation source list.

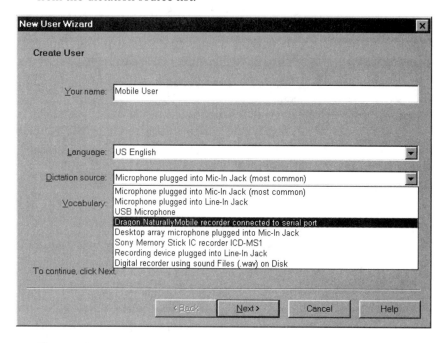

Use the following table as a guide for selecting a dictation source and deciding what to do next.

DICTATION SOURCE	HOW TO PROCEED
Dragon NaturallyMobile recorder connected to serial port	Use the recorder as a microphone attached to your computer with the supplied serial cable. Do not proceed any further with the training instructions in this chapter. Instead, use the instructions on page 132. Training time will be approximately 18 minutes.

DICTATION SOURCE	HOW TO PROCEED
Sony Memory Stick IC Recorder ICD-MS1	Skip to step 5.
Recording device plugged into Line-In Jack	Be sure the recorder is connected to your computer with a cable plugged into your sound card, and proceed to step 4.
Digital recorder using sound files (.wav) on disk (includes the Sony ICD-R100)	Skip to step 5.

4   Follow the instructions in the Adjust Your Volume screens to adjust your analog recorder's volume and check the recorder's audio quality.

5   On the Recording your speech screen, select the text you would like to read from the list of choices. Click View if you want to read the text from the screen. Click Print if you want to send the text to your printer so you can read it while away from your computer.

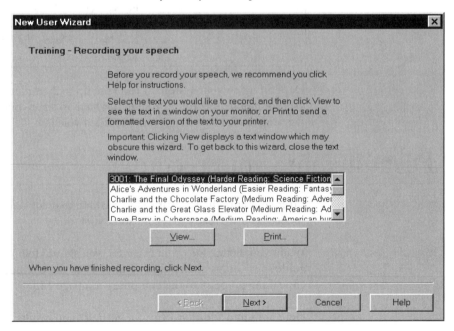

6   After you have recorded approximately 18 minutes of your voice reading the text selection, click Next.

7 The screen that appears and what you do next depends on the recorder type you have selected.

RECORDER TYPE	HOW TO PROCEED
Sony Memory Stick IC Recorder ICD-MS1	Click the "Sony Memory Stick Voice Editor" button and follow the instructions on the screen.
Recording device plugged into Line-In Jack	Be sure that the recorder is connected to the line-in jack on your computer and (optionally) select the Detect end of recording and automatically adapt user files box. If you do this, choose the number of seconds of silence before the wizard assumes that the recording is finished. Then click Start Recording and start your recorder to play back your dictation.
Digital recorder using sound Files (.wav) on Disk	Transfer the .wav file to your computer's hard disk and then use the Browse button to locate the file. If you are not sure how to transfer recorded data to your computer, see the documentation for your recorder. Finally, click Next and follow the instructions on the screen.

8 Depending on your system, it can take up to 20 minutes to adapt your user for mobile recording. You do not have to sit at your computer while the program is adapting to your recorded voice.

Dictating into your recorder

After you train Dragon NaturallySpeaking to recognize your recorded speech, you are ready to record some dictation.

When you dictate into your recorder, you should follow the same guidelines you use when talking directly to the computer. (See "Speaking properly to the computer" on page 12.)

Here are some additional tips for getting good results:

- If you talk directly into a built-in microphone, always hold your recorder at the same distance from your mouth. Some users report that it is easier to rest the recorder on their jaw for the most consistent results. Be sure to hold the recorder at the same distance you used when you dictated the training text.

■ Don't change the recording volume setting on your recorder (if it has one). Keep the same setting you used during training. If the setting changes, check the audio volume and quality again. From the NaturallySpeaking menu, point to Advanced and click Check Audio.

■ Consider connecting your headset microphone to your recorder, rather than talking into the built-in microphone. Using the headset microphone is likely to produce better quality recordings.

The restricted command set

When you are dictating into a recorder, most of the Dragon NaturallySpeaking voice commands cannot be used effectively because they require that you see the results on a computer screen. The restricted command set, however, can be used without visual feedback when you are dictating into your recorder. The following is a list of the commands in the restricted command set:

■ New Paragraph

■ New Line

■ Tab Key

■ Cap [word]

■ All Caps [word]

■ No Caps [word]

■ No Space [word]

■ Caps On/Caps Off

■ All Caps On/All Caps Off

■ No Caps On/No Caps Off

■ No Space On/No Space Off

■ Scratch That

■ Resume With

TIP *"Resume With" is particularly useful when you are using a recorder. It lets you back up if you misspeak or change your mind after dictating a phrase. For more information, see "Backing up as you dictate" on page 101.*

Later, when you transcribe your recorded dictation, you can choose to make Dragon NaturallySpeaking ignore all but the commands in the previous list (or a subset of the list). This prevents potentially damaging recognition errors (for example, a phrase being incorrectly interpreted as the command *"Delete Previous 5 Paragraphs,"* which would actually delete the previous five paragraphs from your transcription). For more information on how to do this, see the section on "The Advanced Settings dialog box" on page 165.

Transcribing recorded dictation

Connecting a recorder to your computer

Before Dragon NaturallySpeaking can transcribe your recorded dictation, you must establish the connection between your recorder or your recorder's memory, and your computer. Use the connection method you used when you created the user adapted to your recorded speech.

The following procedures describe the different methods you use for transcription, depending on the type of recorder you are using. Use the method that is appropriate for your recorder.

Transcribing from the Dragon NaturallyMobile recorder or the Sony Memory Stick IC Recorder ICD-MS1

Dragon NaturallySpeaking has features specifically adapted to work with the Dragon NaturallyMobile recorder and the Sony Memory Stick IC Recorder ICD-MS1. To transfer files from these recorders, use the following procedure.

> **NOTE** *If you are transcribing from a recorder other than the Dragon NaturallyMobile recorder or the Sony Memory Stick IC Recorder ICD-MS1, see "Transcribing dictation from other recorders" on page 163 for instructions.*

To transcribe recorded dictation:

1 Start Dragon NaturallySpeaking. (You don't need to turn the microphone on.)

2 Open the user adapted for your recorded speech. (Click the Users button on the DragonBar, and then click the user name.)

3 From the NaturallySpeaking menu, point to Advanced, and click Transcribe Recording. (If the Extras toolbar is displayed, you can also click the Transcribe button.)

The Transcribe a Recording dialog box opens. (The text next to the large button on the left depends on which recorder you are using. The illustration shows the text for the Sony Memory Stick IC Recorder ICD-MS1.)

4 Click the large button on the left.

If you want to change the target (or destination) window of the transcription, specify which commands Dragon NaturallySpeaking will understand, or the communications port, and click the Advanced button. For a more detailed description of the options see the section "The Advanced Settings dialog box" on page 165.

5 If you are using the Dragon NaturallyMobile recorder, the Select Files for Transcription dialog box opens.

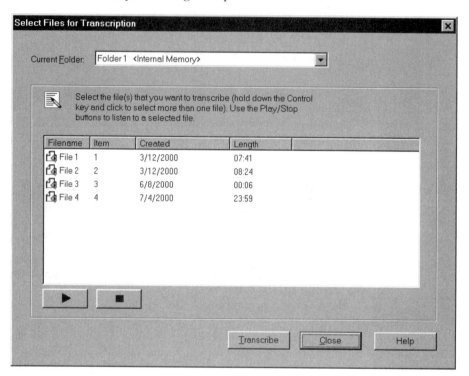

If you are using the Sony Memory Stick IC Recorder ICD-MS1, the Sony Memory Stick Voice Editor dialog box opens.

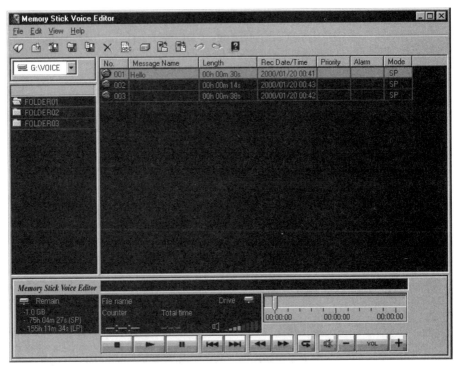

6 If you are using the Dragon NaturallyMobile recorder, select the file or files you want to transcribe, and click the Transcribe button. If you are using the Sony Memory Stick IC Recorder ICD-MS1, select the file or files on the Memory Stick Voice Editor screen and, from the File menu, click Voice Recognition (you can also click the Voice Recognition tool on the toolbar).

Transcribing dictation from other recorders

To transcribe recorded dictation from recorders other than the Dragon NaturallyMobile recorder and the Sony Memory Stick IC Recorder ICD-MS1, use the following procedure.

To transcribe recorded dictation:

1 Start Dragon NaturallySpeaking. (You don't need to turn the microphone on.)

2 Open the user adapted for your recorded speech. (Click the Users button on the DragonBar and then click the user name.)

From the NaturallySpeaking menu, point to Advanced, and click Transcribe Recording. (If the Extras toolbar is displayed, you can also click the Transcribe button.)

The Transcribe from dialog box opens.

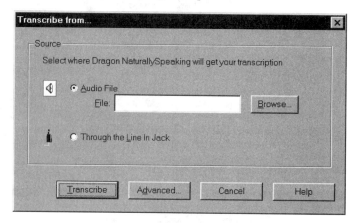

NOTE *You can also open the Transcribe from dialog box by clicking the Other Source button on the Transcribe a Recording dialog box when using either the Sony Memory Stick IC Recorder ICD-MS1 or the Dragon NaturallyMobile recorder.*

3 Use the Transcribe from dialog box in the following manner to select the source of the dictation you want Dragon NaturallySpeaking to transcribe, as well as other options that control the transcription:

■ If the dictation source is a wave file, click Browse to locate the file.

■ If you are playing back recorded dictation through the Line In jack, transcription stops automatically by default as soon as the computer hears ten seconds of silence.

■ If you want to change the final destination of the transcription, specify which commands Dragon NaturallySpeaking will understand, or increase or decrease the number of seconds after which the transcription automatically stops (Line In recorders only), click the Advanced button. For a more detailed description of the options see the section "The Advanced Settings dialog box" on page 165.

4 To begin transcription, click Transcribe.

5 If your dictation source is "Recording device plugged into Line-In Jack," press the Play button on your recorder.

Your recorded speech should appear on the screen. If text doesn't appear, see the section, "Troubleshooting" on page 167.

TIP *When you are transcribing into the DragonPad, you can use your computer for other purposes while you wait for Dragon NaturallySpeaking to finish.*

The Advanced Settings dialog box

The Advanced Settings dialog box allows you to change how Dragon NaturallySpeaking transcribes the dictation from your recorder. The options you see when you open the dialog box depend on the type of recorder you are using. The illustration shows the Advanced Settings dialog box that appears when you are transcribing from the Dragon NaturallyMobile recorder.

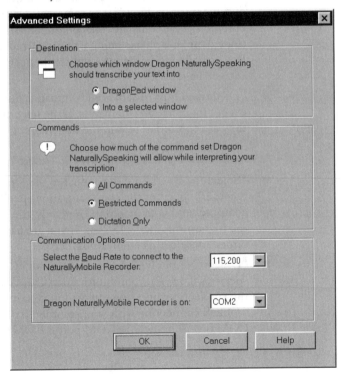

The following sections describe the options on the Advanced Settings dialog box:

Destination

You can choose to specify that the recording should be transcribed into the DragonPad window or into a selected window you click in after closing the Transcribe Recording dialog box. Make sure the window you select accepts text.

Commands

You can choose either the All Commands, Restricted Commands, or Dictation Only option.

■ "All Commands" enables all Dragon NaturallySpeaking commands during transcription. Any command recognized in the recording is carried out.

■ "Restricted Commands" disables all but the restricted command set during transcription. If other commands are recognized, they are entered as text. This prevents potentially damaging misrecognitions (for example, a phrase being misrecognized as "Delete Previous Paragraph"). For more information about the restricted command set, see page 159.

■ "Dictation Only" disables all commands during transcription, except for dictation commands. If the recording contains commands, they are entered as text in the document.

Communication Options (for the Dragon NaturallyMobile recorder only)

■ "Select the Baud Rate to connect to the Dragon NaturallyMobile recorder" specifies the communication speed between your computer and your recorder. Generally, the speed should be set to the highest number (115,200). If you are having communication errors, try selecting a lower number.

■ "Dragon NaturallyMobile recorder is on <Com Port Number>" specifies the serial communications (COM) port that corresponds to the connector where you plugged in your recorder. If you have a problem connecting with your recorder, try selecting a different COM port. The default COM port is COM1.

Miscellaneous Options (for Line Input recorders only)

"When using a Line Input recorder, stop transcribing after <N> seconds of silence" instructs Dragon NaturallySpeaking to finish transcribing a recording after it detects a certain number of seconds of silence. You can enter any value between 1 and 99 seconds, but it should be long enough that Dragon NaturallySpeaking will not think you have finished when you are only pausing. Then, when you are dictating, be sure not to pause for more than the number of seconds you choose. At the end of your dictation, be sure that you record silence for at least that number of seconds.

Troubleshooting

If text doesn't appear on the screen, check the following:

- If you are using the Transcribe Recording dialog box, did you click in a window after closing it? If you aren't transcribing in the DragonPad window, you must click in the window in which you want the text to appear.

- If you selected Through the Line-In Jack as your source, did you remember to press the play button on your recorder? Is your recorder properly connected to the computer?

- Are you playing the right part of the recording? Listen to the source file to make sure it contains dictation.

- If you are using an analog recorder, have you changed the volume setting on your recorder since running training? If so, check the audio volume and quality again. From the NaturallySpeaking menu, point to Advanced, and click Check Audio.

- Is your recorder working properly? Check the power source. If you are using a battery, make sure it is fully charged.

- If you are transcribing a wave file, make sure the file is in the following format: PCM, 11,025 Hz, 16 Bit, Mono.

- If you are having difficulties transcribing text from the Dragon recorder, consult the troubleshooting section of the online Help files for the Voice It® Link® software. See the procedure "To install Voice It Link (for the Dragon NaturallyMobile recorder)" on page 155 for information on installing Voice It Link.

Correcting mistakes

After Dragon NaturallySpeaking transcribes your dictation, make sure you correct any mistakes. To help you check for mistakes, you can play back your recorded voice as you read what Dragon NaturallySpeaking transcribed. Listening to your dictation as you read the transcription will help you identify misrecognized words or phrases.

To start playback:

Select the text you want to play back and click the button on the Extras toolbar of the DragonBar (or press CTRL+SHIFT+S).

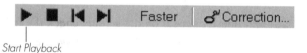

Start Playback

> **NOTE** *Because of memory constraints, Dragon NaturallySpeaking can play back only your last 100 utterances (defined by the pauses in your speech). To increase the amount of transcribed text you can play back, try speaking in longer phrases without pausing for a breath, or increase the "Pause between phrases" setting. (From the NaturallySpeaking menu, point to Advanced, and click Options. In the Options dialog box, click the Miscellaneous tab.)*

To stop playback:

To stop playback, do any of the following:

■ Click the Stop Playback ■ button on the Extras toolbar.

■ Click anywhere in the document window.

■ Press the ESC key.

To skip words or go faster or slower:

■ To skip forward a few words, click the Skip Forward button ▶| .

■ To skip backward a few words, click the Skip Backward button |◀ .

■ To go faster or slower, click the Faster/Slower button Faster or press the right or left arrow keys.

To correct a mistake:

To correct a word or phrase, select it and then click the Correct button Correction… or press the minus (-) key on the numeric keypad.

TIP *One of the most effective ways to proof and correct a transcription is simply to select the entire transcription and play it back. During playback, you can press the right arrow key to speed up the playback and the left arrow key to slow it down. When you see a mistake, just press the down arrow key to open the Correction dialog box.*

When you are working in the Correction dialog box, click Play Back to play the dictation that goes with the words in the Correction dialog box. Then edit the text to match what you said.

TIP *You can set up Dragon NaturallySpeaking to play back dictation automatically whenever you open the Correction dialog box. From the NaturallySpeaking menu, point to Advanced, and click Options. In the Options dialog box, click the Correction tab and select "Automatic playback on correction."*

Using the Dragon NaturallyMobile recorder as a microphone

If you have a Dragon NaturallyMobile recorder, you can use it as a microphone when it is connected to a computer with the supplied serial cable.

To use the recorder as a microphone:

1 Open the user you created for the Dragon NaturallyMobile recorder, if it is not already open. (On the DragonBar click the Users button and click the name of the user.)

2 Make sure the recorder is connected to the serial port of your computer.

3 Click the Microphone button on the DragonBar so the microphone is on (🎤).

4 Wait until the recorder display reads "Mic On." This takes about two or three seconds after you click on the Microphone button.

5 Begin speaking, holding the built-in microphone of the recorder almost touching the corner of your mouth and a bit to the side. Do not hold the recorder so that the microphone is directly in front of your mouth.

Hold the recorder so that the built-in microphone is at the side of your mouth, not in front of it.

6 When you have finished, click the Microphone button again so the microphone is off.

> **NOTE** Turning off the microphone in this way does not turn off the recorder. To conserve your batteries, turn off the recorder by pressing the Power button.

Dragon NaturallySpeaking Version 5 Commands List

T his appendix lists the Dragon NaturallySpeaking commands. Most of the commands listed here are described in detail elsewhere in this guide. For more information about commands, follow the page references provided throughout the appendix.

Which commands work in which programs?

Some commands work only in certain types of programs. For example, *"Set Font Bold"* works only in programs where you can make text bold. Special symbols in this appendix and in the online Help indicate where you can expect a command to work.

● A circle means that the command works in most applications.

■ A square means that the command works in the following (word processing) programs:

- ■ DragonPad
- ■ Lotus Notes 5
- ■ Microsoft Word 97 or Word 2000 (including the Word editor in Outlook)
- ■ WordPad
- ■ WordPerfect 8 or 9

▲ A triangle means that in most programs, the command works on what you just said. For example, you can say "*Scratch That*" to erase what you just said.

Commands marked with a triangle also work on selected text in programs that support *Select-and-Say* (listed below). In these programs, for example, you can say "*Cap That*" to capitalize the first letter of selected text.

◆ A diamond means that the command works *only* in the Select-and-Say programs listed below. For more information on Select-and-Say, see "Using Select-and-Say" on page 90.

PROGRAMS THAT SUPPORT SELECT-AND-SAY	
DragonPad	Microsoft Word 97 or Word 2000
WordPerfect 8 or 9	Lotus Notes 5.0
Microsoft Chat 2.1 or 2.5	GoldMine 4.0
Internet Explorer 4 or 5	Microsoft Outlook Express 5
WordPad	Notepad
Microsoft Outlook 97, 98, or 2000 with plain text or Outlook Rich Text selected, or using Microsoft Word 2000 as the editor	

TIP *If you say a command that does not work in the program you are using, the DragonBar may show a message: for example, "Formatting commands cannot be used here."*

Commands listed in the sections on e-mail, Lotus Notes, and Internet Explorer do not have symbols, because they are designed to work only in those applications.

Controlling the microphone

SAY	TO
● Go to Sleep	Make the microphone stop listening temporarily.
● Wake Up	Reactivate the microphone when it's sleeping.
● Microphone Off	Turn the microphone off. (You cannot turn it back on by voice.)

Controlling the DragonBar

SAY	TO
● Click NaturallySpeaking or NaturallySpeaking	Open the NaturallySpeaking main menu on the DragonBar (or on the DragonPad if it is active).
● Start DragonPad	Start the DragonPad word processor.
● Click Users or Users	Open the NaturallySpeaking Users menu.
● Give Me Help	Display Dragon NaturallySpeaking online Help.
● What Can I Say or Spoken Commands	Display the Command List in online Help.

Adding paragraphs, lines, and spaces

SAY	TO
● New Line	Press the ENTER key once.
● New Paragraph	Press the ENTER key twice. (Capitalizes the next word automatically.)
● Tab Key	Press the TAB key.
● Space Bar	Press the space bar.

Selecting text

Selecting specific words

SAY	TO
◆ Select *glass*	Select a specific word or words that are visible on screen. In this example, select *glass*.
◆ Select Again	Select the same text again but in a different place, which is also visible on screen.
◆ **US/Canada:** Select *It was* Through *night* ◆ **Other Dialects:** Select *It was* To *night*	Select a range of words visible on screen. In this example, select *It was a dark and stormy night*.
◆ Select That	Select the last thing you said.
◆ Unselect That	Unselect selected text.

For more information about these commands, see "Selecting text" on page 90.

Selecting an entire line or paragraph

SAY	THEN *(one)*	THEN *(one)*
● Select	Next	Line
	Forward	2...20 Lines
	Previous	Paragraph
	Back	2 Paragraphs
	Last	2...20 Paragraphs

For more information about these commands, see "Selecting an entire paragraph or line" on page 94.

Selecting a word or character

SAY	THEN (one)	THEN (one)
● Select	Next	Word
	Forward	2 Words
	Previous	2...20 Words
	Back	Character
	Last	4 Characters
		2...20 Characters

TIP *You can also say "Select Word," "Select Line," or "Select Character."*

For more information about these commands, see "Selecting a word or character" on page 94.

Selecting a document

SAY	TO
● Select Document/ Select All	Select all the text in your document.

Correcting text

SAY	TO
▲ Select That	Select the last thing you said and display the Quick Correct list (by default; you can choose to display the Correction dialog box instead).
▲ Correct That	Correct either the last thing you said or selected text.
◆ Correct *carefully*	Correct a specific word or words that are visible on screen. In this example, correct the word *carefully.*
◆ **US/Canada:** Correct *It was* Through *night* ◆ **Other Dialects:** Correct *It was* To *night*	Correct a range of words that are visible on screen. In this example, correct *It was a dark and stormy night.*
● Spell	Spell a word (brings up the Correction dialog box).
● Spell *g-l-a-s-s*	Spell the next word, in this example, *glass.*
▲ Spell That *g-l-a-s-s*	Correct either the last thing you said or selected text by spelling the correction, in this example, *glass.* See the list in the next section, "Correction dialog box commands," for spelling tips.

For more information about these commands, see "Correcting recognition mistakes" on page 15.

Correction dialog box commands

SAY	TO
Choose 2	Select an alternative from the numbered list and enter it in your document. You can say any number that appears in the list.
Select 4	Select an alternative from the numbered list for editing. You can say any number that appears in the list.
Scratch That	Erase the dictated text in the Correction dialog box.

The standard commands for moving the insertion point and selecting text will also work here. For more information about these commands, see "Correcting recognition mistakes" on page 15.

Spelling in the Correction dialog box

When you are spelling in the Correction dialog box, this is what you can say:

- letters (a–z)
- International Communications Alphabet (alpha, bravo, and so on)
- numbers (0–9)
- punctuation
- "Cap" (to capitalize the next letter)
- "Double" (to enter the next letter twice, for example, *"Double a"*)
- "Space Bar" or "space" (to insert a space)
- "Backspace"
- "apostrophe ess"
- special characters (such as @, *, £, ©, and é)

See the following sections for the International Communications Alphabet and lists of special characters.

International Communications Alphabet

When spelling in the Correction dialog box, you can use the International Communications Alphabet to enter letters. For a complete list of alphabet choices, see the online Help.

FOR	SAY	FOR	SAY
a	Alpha	n	November
b	Bravo	o	Oscar
c	Charlie	p	Papa
d	Delta	q	Quebec
e	Echo	r	Romeo
f	Foxtrot	s	Sierra
g	Golf	t	Tango
h	Hotel	u	Uniform
i	India	v	Victor
j	Juliet	w	Whiskey
k	Kilo	x	X-ray
l	Lima	y	Yankee
m	Mike	z	Zulu

Publishing symbols

When spelling in the Correction dialog box, you can enter the following special characters by voice. (If the program has trouble recognizing a character, try using the longest available spoken form.)

TO ENTER	SAY
™	trademark sign *or* trademark
©	copyright sign *or* copyright
®	registered trademark sign *or* registered trademark *or* registered sign *or* registered
†	dagger
‡	double dagger
¶	paragraph sign *or* paragraph
§	section sign *or* section
—	em dash

TO ENTER	SAY
–	en dash
-	soft hyphen
(Nonbreaking space)	nonbreaking space *or* nonbreakable space *or* no break space *or* unbreakable space

Currency symbols

When spelling in the Correction dialog box, you can enter the following special characters by voice. (If the program has trouble recognizing a character, try using the longest available spoken form.)

TO ENTER	SAY
$	dollar sign *or* dollar
¢	cent sign/cent
£	**US/Canada:** pound sterling sign **Other Dialects:** pound sign *or* pound
¥	yen sign *or* yen
€ (or EUR)*	euro sign *or* euro
ƒ	guilder sign *or* guilder
¤	general currency *or* general currency sign international currency *or* international currency sign

* Dragon NaturallySpeaking uses EUR as the default for the euro symbol. For the program to recognize "euro" in symbol form, you must change the Euro option in the Dragon NaturallySpeaking Options dialog box. From the NaturallySpeaking menu, point to Advanced, click Options, and then click the Formatting tab. Type the euro symbol in the "Euro symbol or abbreviation" box.

Accented and international characters

When spelling in the Correction dialog box, you can enter the following special characters by voice. (If the program has trouble recognizing a character, try using the longest available spoken form.)

TO ENTER	SAY
´ (acute)	accent acute *or* acute
` (grave)	accent grave *or* grave *or* backquote
~ (tilde)	centered tilde *or* accent tilde *or* tilde
¨ (umlaut)	accent umlaut *or* dieresis
^ (circumflex)	accent circumflex *or* circumflex

TO ENTER	SAY
¸ (cedilla)	cedilla *or* accent cedilla
á, Á, é, É, í, Í, ó, Ó, ú, Ú, ý, Ý	a accent acute (or "a acute") Cap e accent acute (or "Cap e acute") and so on
à, À, È, è, ì, Ì, ò, Ò, ù, Ù	a accent grave (or "a grave") Cap e accent grave (or "Cap e grave") and so on
ã, Ã, ñ, Ñ, õ, Õ	a accent tilde (or "a tilde") Cap n accent tilde (or "Cap n tilde") and so on
ä, Ä, ë, Ë, ï, Ï, ö, Ö, ü, Ü, ÿ, Ÿ	a accent umlaut (or "a umlaut") Cap e accent umlaut (or "Cap e umlaut") and so on
â, Â, ê, Ê, î, Î, ô, Ô, û, Û	a accent circumflex (or "a circumflex") Cap o accent circumflex (or "Cap o circumflex") and so on
ç, Ç	c accent cedilla (or "c cedilla") Cap c accent cedilla (or "Cap c cedilla")
å, Å	a angstrom Cap a angstrom
¡	inverted exclamation point *or* inverted exclamation mark
¿	inverted question mark
«	open-angle-quotes *or* begin-angle-quotes
»	close-angle-quotes *or* end-angle-quotes
ß	eszet *or* German sharp *or* German sharp s *or* sharp s
œ	oe ligature *or* ligature oe *or* oe diphthong
æ	ae ligature *or* ae diphthong *or* ligature ae
ð	Icelandic eth *or* eth
þ	Icelandic thorn *or* thorn
°	masculine ordinal
ª	feminine ordinal
š	s wedge
„	double comma

Mathematical symbols

When spelling in the Correction dialog box, you can enter the following special characters by voice. (If the program has trouble recognizing a character, try using the longest available spoken form.)

TO ENTER	SAY
¼	one quarter sign *or* one quarter *or* quarter sign *or* quarter
½	one half sign *or* one half *or* half sign *or* half
¾	three quarters sign *or* three quarters
×	multiply sign *or* multiply *or* times sign *or* times *or* multiplication sign
÷	divide sign *or* divide
±	plus or minus sign *or* plus or minus *or* plus minus sign *or* plus minus
‰	per thousand *or* per mille
¦	broken vertical bar
¬	logical not sign *or* logical not *or* not sign *or* not
¯	macron sign *or* macron
°	degree sign *or* degree
¹	superscript 1
²	superscript 2 *or* squared *or* square
³	superscript 3 *or* cubed *or* cube
µ	Greek mu *or* micro
ø	o slash
·	centered-dot *or* middle-dot *or* center-dot
،	alternate-comma

Erasing and undoing

SAY	TO
● Delete That	Delete selected text. *(For more information, see "Deleting specific words" on page 101.)*
● Backspace	Press the BACKSPACE key. To press it more than once, say *Backspace 2, Backspace 3*, and so on (up to 20).
● Undo That *or* Undo Last Action	Undo the last action.
▲ Scratch That	Erase the last thing you said or selected text. You can say "Scratch That" up to 10 times to keep erasing previous words or phrases. *(For more information, see "Deleting the last words you dictated" on page 100.)*
◆ Resume With *Dear Susan*	Search backward to find a specific word or words, so you can continue dictating from that point. In this example, resume dictating with *Dear Susan*. *(For more information, see "Backing up as you dictate" on page 101.)*

Deleting the next or previous line or paragraph

SAY	THEN *(one)*	THEN *(one)*
● Delete	Next	Paragraph
	Forward	2 Paragraphs
	Previous	2...20 Paragraphs
	Back	Line
	Last	2...20 Lines

For more information about these commands, see "Deleting the next or previous paragraph or line" on page 102.

Deleting the next or previous word or character

SAY	THEN *(one)*	THEN *(one)*
● Delete	Next	Word
	Forward	Character
	Previous	2 Words
	Back	3 Characters
	Last	2...20 Words
		2...20 Characters

For more information about these commands, see "Deleting the next or previous word or character" on page 102.

Moving around in a document

Going to the top or bottom of a document

SAY	THEN *(one)*
● Go to	Top
● Move to	Top of Document
	Beginning of Document
	Start of Document
	Bottom
	Bottom of Document
	End of Document

Going to the top or bottom of a page

SAY	TO
Page Up	Move up one page (equivalent to pressing the PAGE UP key).
Page Down	Move down one page (equivalent to pressing the PAGE DOWN key).

For more information about these commands, see "Going to the top or bottom of a page or document" on page 88.

Going to the beginning or end of a line

SAY	THEN *(one)*
● Go to	Beginning of Line
● Move to	Start of Line
	End of Line

For more information about these commands, see "Going to the beginning or end of a line" on page 88.

Placing the insertion point before or after a specific word

SAY	TO
◆ Insert Before *glass*	Place the insertion point before a specific word or words that are visible on screen. In this example, select *glass*.
◆ Insert After *glass*	Place the insertion point after a specific word or words that are visible on screen. In this example, select *glass*.
◆ Insert Before That	Place the insertion point before selected text that is visible on screen.
◆ Insert After That	Place the insertion point after selected text that is visible on screen.

For more information about these commands, see "Placing the insertion point before or after a specific word" on page 88.

Moving up or down a paragraph

SAY	THEN *(one)*	THEN *(one)*
● Move	Up	a Paragraph (or "1 Paragraph")
	Back	2 Paragraphs
	Down	3 Paragraphs
	Forward	2...20 Paragraphs

For example, you can say "*Move Up a Paragraph*" or "*Move Down Six Paragraphs.*" For more information about these commands, see "Moving up or down a paragraph or line" on page 89.

Moving up or down a line

SAY	THEN (one)	THEN (one)
● Move	Up	a Line (or *1 Line*)
	Back	2 Lines
	Down	3 Lines
	Forward	*2...20* Lines

For example, you can say "*Move Up a Line*" or "*Move Down Six Lines.*" For more information about these commands, see "Moving right or left a word or character" on page 90.

Moving right or left a word

SAY	THEN (one)	THEN (one)
● Move	Right	a Word (or *1 Word*)
	Forward	2 Words
	Left	4 Words
	Back	*2...20* Words

For example, you can say "*Move Right a Word*" or "*Move Forward Six Words.*" For more information about these commands, see "Moving right or left a word or character" on page 90.

Moving right or left a character

SAY	THEN (one)	THEN (one)
● Move	Right	a Character (or *1 Character*)
	Forward	2 Characters
	Left	4 Characters
	Back	*2...20* Characters
		2...20
		2...20

For example, you can say "*Move Right a Character*" or "*Move Left Six.*" For more information about these commands, see "Moving right or left a word or character" on page 90.

Copying, cutting, and pasting text

SAY	TO
● Copy Selection	Copy selected text to the Clipboard.
● Cut Selection	Cut selected text.
▲ Copy That	Copy the last thing you said or selected text to the Clipboard.
▲ Cut That	Cut the last thing you said or selected text.
● Paste That	Paste the contents of the Clipboard.
● Copy All to Clipboard	Copy all the text in your document to the Clipboard.

For more information about these commands, see "Copying, cutting, and pasting text" on page 95.

Capitalizing text

Capitalizing or uncapitalizing text already in your document

SAY	TO
▲ Cap That *or* Capitalize That *or* ▲ Format That Capitals *or* Format That Initial Caps *or* Format That Cap *or* Format That Caps	Capitalize either the last thing you said or selected text.
▲ All Caps That *or* Format That All Caps *or* Format That Uppercase	Make either the last thing you said or selected text all capitals.
▲ No Caps That *or* Format That No Caps *or* Format That Lowercase	Make either the last thing you said or selected text all lowercase.

For more information about these commands, see "Capitalizing (or uncapitalizing) text already in your document" on page 97.

Capitalizing or uncapitalizing the next word you say

SAY	TO
● Cap *glass*	Start the next word with a capital, in this example, *Glass.*
● All Caps *glass*	Type the next word in all capitals, in this example, *GLASS.*
● No Caps *Jack*	Type the next word in all lowercase, in this example, *jack.*
● No Space *glass*	Type the next word without a space before it; for example, *window No Space glass = windowglass.*

For more information about these commands, see "Capitalizing text" on page 95.

Capitalizing or uncapitalizing consecutive words

SAY	TO
● Caps On	Turn initial caps on.
● Caps Off	Turn initial caps off.
● All Caps On	Turn all capitals on.
● All Caps Off	Turn all capitals off.
● No Caps On	Turn all lowercase on.
● No Caps Off	Turn all lowercase off.
● No Space On	Turn no spaces on.
● No Space Off	Turn no spaces off.

For more information about these commands, see "Capitalizing text" on page 95 and "Compounding words as you dictate" on page 69.

Hyphenating or compounding text

SAY	TO
▲ Hyphenate That *or* Format That With Hyphens	Hyphenate either the last thing you said or selected text.
▲ Compound That *or* Format That Without Spaces	Compound either the last thing you said or selected text.

For more information about these commands, see "Adding hyphens later" on page 68 and "Compounding words later" on page 70.

Formatting text

Adding or removing bold, italics, and underlining

SAY	TO
▪ Bold That	Apply bold to either the last thing you said or selected text.
▪ Italicize That	Apply italics to either the last thing you said or selected text.
▪ Underline That	Apply underlining to either the last thing you said or selected text.
▪ Restore That *or* Format That Plain *or* Format That Normal *or* Format That Regular	Remove formatting from selected text.

For more information about these commands, see "Adding (or removing) bold, italics, and underlining" on page 100.

Changing font face

SAY *(one)*	THEN *(one)*
■ Set Font	Times
■ Format That	Times New Roman
	Arial
	Courier
	Courier New

For more information about these commands, see "Changing font face" on page 98.

Changing font size

SAY *(one)*	THEN *(one)*
■ Set Size	8
■ Format That Size	10 point
■ Set Font Size	12
	any point size from 4 to 100, as well as 120

For more information about these commands, see "Changing font size" on page 98.

Changing font style

SAY *(one)*	THEN *(one)*
■ Set Font	Bold
■ Format That	Italics
	Underline
	Strikeout
	Plain *or* Plain Text *or* Normal *or* Regular

For more information about these commands, see "Changing font style" on page 99.

Changing a combination of font face, size, and style

SAY (one)	THEN (one)	THEN (one)	THEN (one)
■ Set Font	Times	8	Bold
■ Format That	Times New Roman	10 point	Italics
	Arial	12	Underline
	Courier	*any point size from 4 to 100, as well as 120*	Plain *or* Plain Text *or* Normal *or* Regular

For more information about these commands, see "Changing a combination of font face, size, and style" on page 99.

Aligning text

SAY	TO
■ Center That *or* Format That Centered	Center the current paragraph.
■ Left Align That *or* Format That Left Aligned	Left align the current paragraph.
■ Right Align That *or* Format That Right Aligned	Right align the current paragraph.

For more information about these commands, see "Aligning text" on page 100.

Entering numbers

TO ENTER	SAY
5	five *or* numeral five
23	twenty three
179	one hundred seventy nine *or* one seventy nine
5423	five thousand four hundred and twenty three
5,423	five [comma] four twenty three
12,537	twelve thousand five hundred and thirty seven
142,015	one hundred and forty two thousand and fifteen
35.23	thirty five [point] two three
0.03	**All Dialects:** zero [point] zero three **Outside US/Canada:** nought [point] nought three
43.28%	forty three [point] twenty eight [percent sign]
22 January 1999	twenty two January nineteen ninety nine
April 9, 2001	April nine comma two thousand and one
14/07/85	fourteen [slash] oh seven [slash] eighty five
6/12/00	six [slash] twelve [slash] double oh *or* six [slash] twelve [slash] double zero NOTE: *If you say "oh oh," you must then say "Format That Number" to remove the extra space.*
1/22/2000	one [slash] twenty-two [slash] two thousand
8:30	eight [colon] thirty
4:45 am	four forty five a m
10:22 pm	ten twenty two p m
5:00 PM	five o'clock p m
£ 45	**US/Canada:** pound sterling sign forty five **Other Dialects:** forty five pounds
$99.50	ninety nine dollars and fifty cents
£ 5 million	**US/Canada:** pound sterling sign five million **Other Dialects:** five million pounds
$3.9 billion	**US/Canada:** three point nine billion dollars **Other Dialects:** dollar sign three point nine billion
1/2	one half
1/4	one fourth *or* one quarter

TO ENTER	SAY
15/16	fifteen sixteenths *or* fifteen over sixteen
3 7/8	three and seven eighths *or* three and seven over eight
9/12	nine [slash] twelve *or* nine over twelve
5 3/56	five [space bar] three [slash] fifty six
130/70	one thirty over seventy
V	Roman five
XXIV	Roman twenty Roman four

Telephone numbers

TO ENTER	SAY
617-965-5200	six one seven nine six five fifty two hundred
1-800-555-1212	one eight hundred five five five one two one two
(617) 965-5200	[open parenthesis] six one seven [close parenthesis] nine six five five two hundred
1-212-555-1212	one two one two five five five one two one two
(01628) 894150	open parenthesis oh one six two eight close parenthesis space bar eight nine four one five oh
027 629 8944	oh two seven space bar six two nine space bar eight nine four four
61-7-4695-2055	six one hyphen seven hyphen four six nine five hyphen two zero five five
(65) 2778590	open parenthesis six five close parenthesis two seven seven eight five nine zero

NOTE *You can say North American phone numbers (of 7, 10, or 11 digits) without hyphens by pausing briefly between each group of numbers. To dictate other phone numbers, including European phone numbers, you must say all the punctuation, including the hyphens. This also applies to eight-digit numbers starting with 0 or 1 (for example, 1-965-5200). For more information, see "Telephone numbers" on page 80.*

Postal and ZIP codes

TO ENTER	SAY
02460	oh two four six zero
02460-1458	oh two four six zero [hyphen] one four five eight NOTE: the hyphen is not optional.
K1A 0M5	Postal Code k one a oh m five or Postal Code kilo one alpha zero mike five
X0A 0H0	Postal code x oh a oh h o or Postal code x-ray zero alpha zero hotel zero
SL7 1LW	Post Code s l seven one l w or Post Code sierra lima seven one lima whiskey

NOTE *You can say U.S. five- or nine-digit ZIP codes naturally, as a group of numbers; you must dictate the hyphen for nine-digit ZIP+4 codes. To dictate Canadian or U.K. postal codes, you must say "Postal Code" or Post Code" followed by the numbers and letters (you don't have to dictate the space or capitalization).*

For more information about entering numbers, see "Dictating numbers" on page 76.

Changing number format

SAY	TO
▲ Format That Number	Convert a number from text to numeric format (for example, convert *one hundred* to *100*).
▲ Format That Spelled Out	Convert a number from numeric to text format (for example, convert *100* to *one hundred*).
● Start Numbers Mode/ Numbers Mode On	Tell Dragon NaturallySpeaking to recognize all your dictation as numbers, typed as numerals.
● Stop Numbers Mode/ Numbers Mode Off	Resume normal dictation of text and numbers.

For more information about these commands, see "Dictating numbers" on page 76.

Entering punctuation and special characters

TO ENTER	SAY	TO ENTER	SAY
&	ampersand *or* and sign	*	asterisk
'	apostrophe	's	apostrophe s
@	at sign	`	backquote
'	open single quote *or* begin single quote	'	close single quote *or* end single quote
"	open quote open quotes *or* begin quote *or* begin quotes	"	close quote *or* close quotes *or* end quote *or* end quotes
\	backslash	/	slash *or* forward slash
:(space)	colon	:	numeric colon
,(space)	comma	,	numeric comma
^	caret	—	dash
.	dot *or* point	.	**US/Canada:** period **Other Dialects:** full stop
$	dollar sign	...	ellipsis
=	equal sign	€	euro sign/euro
!	exclamation point *or* exclamation mark	-	hyphen *or* numeric hyphen
{	open curly bracket *or* left curly bracket **US/Canada:** open brace *or* left brace	}	close curly bracket *or* right curly bracket **US/Canada:** close brace *or* right brace
[	open square bracket *or* left square bracket **US/Canada:** open bracket *or* left bracket	]	close square bracket *or* right square bracket **US/Canada:** close bracket *or* right bracket

TO ENTER	SAY	TO ENTER	SAY
(	**All Dialects:** open parenthesis *or* left parenthesis **US/Canada:** open paren *or* left paren **Other Dialects:** open bracket *or* left bracket	)	**All Dialects:** close parenthesis *or* right parenthesis **US/Canada:** close paren *or* right paren **Other Dialects:** close bracket *or* right bracket
<	open angle bracket	<	less than
>	close angle bracket	>	greater than
-	minus sign	#	number sign *or* hash sign *or* sharp sign **US/Canada:** number sign *or* pound *or* pound sign
%	percent sign	+	plus sign
£	**US/Canada:** pound sterling sign **Other Dialects:** pound sign *or* pound	?	question mark
§	section sign	;	semicolon
(space)	space bar	(tab)	tab key
~	tilde	_	underscore
		vertical bar	:-(	frowny face
:-)	smiley face	;-)	winky face

Playing back and reading text

Playing back dictation

SAY	TO
■ Play That Back *or* Play That *or* Play Selection	Play back the last thing you said or selected text.
■ Play Back Line	Play back dictation for the current line.
■ Play Back Paragraph	Play back dictation for the current paragraph.
■ Play Back Document	Play back dictation for the whole document.
■ Play Back Screen	Play back dictation for the text in view.
■ Play Back to Here *or* Play Back Up to Here	Play back dictation from the top of the document window to the insertion point.
■ Play Back from Here *or* Play Back Down from Here	Play back dictation from the insertion point to the bottom of the document window.

Dictation playback is available for Dragon NaturallySpeaking Preferred and higher editions. For more information about these commands, see "Playing back your dictation" on page 23.

Using Text-to-Speech

SAY	TO
■ Read Line	Read back the current line.
■ Read Paragraph	Read back the current paragraph.
■ Read Document	Read back the whole document.
■ Read Screen	Read back the text in view.
■ Read to Here *or* Read Up to Here	Read back from the top of the document window to the insertion point.
■ Read from Here *or* Read Down from Here	Read back from the insertion point to the bottom of the document window.

Text-to-speech is available for Dragon NaturallySpeaking Preferred and higher editions. For more information about these commands, see "Using text-to-speech" on page 28.

Working with your desktop and windows

Starting programs and opening documents and folders

SAY	TO
● Start *Calculator*	Start a program on your Windows Start menu or desktop, in this example, *Calculator.*
● Start Mail	Start your default e-mail program.
● Start *proposal.doc*	Open a document on your Windows Start menu or desktop, in this example, *proposal.doc.*
● Start *My Documents*	Open a folder on your Windows Start menu or desktop, in this example, *My Documents.*
● Click *Start or* Click *Start Menu*	Open a menu, in this example, the *Start* menu.
● Give Me Help	Open Dragon NaturallySpeaking online Help.
● What Can I Say	Open Dragon NaturallySpeaking online Help to the Command List.

For more information about these commands, see "Starting programs" on page 104 and "Opening documents and folders" on page 105.

Switching windows

SAY	TO
● Switch to *Internet Explorer*	Switch to a different program window, in this example, *Internet Explorer.*
● Switch to Previous Window	Switch to the previous window (equivalent to pressing ALT+TAB).
● Switch to Next Window	Switch to the next window (equivalent to pressing ALT+SHIFT+TAB).
● Switch to DragonPad	Switch to the DragonPad window.

For more information about these commands, see "Switching between open windows" on page 106.

Opening and closing menus

SAY	TO
● Click *File or File*	Open a menu or activate a menu command, in this example, the *File* menu.
● Cancel	Close an open menu.

For more information about these commands, see "Opening and closing menus" on page 107.

Selecting buttons, tabs, and options

SAY	TO
● Click *OK or OK*	Activate a button or option, in this example, *OK*.
● Click *Properties or Properties*	Activate a tab in a tabbed dialog box, in this example, the *Properties* tab.
● Go to Next Tab *or* Move to Next Tab *or* Click Next Tab *or* Next Tab	Switch to the next tab in a tabbed dialog box.
● Go to Previous Tab *or* Move to Previous Tab *or* Click Previous Tab *or* Previous Tab	Switch to the previous tab in a tabbed dialog box.

For more information about these commands, see "Selecting buttons, tabs, and options" on page 108.

Resizing and closing windows

SAY	TO
● Click Maximize	Maximize the active window.
● Click Minimize	Minimize the active window.
● Click Restore	Restore the active window to its previous size.
● Click Close	Close the active window.
● Click Control Menu	Open the Control menu for the active window.
● Click System Menu	Open the System menu for the active window.

For more information about these commands, see "Resizing and closing windows" on page 110.

E-mail commands

The following commands work only when you are in a supported e-mail program. For more information, see "Working with E-mail" on page 119.

Mailbox commands

SAY	TO
Check For New Mail *or* Check For Mail *or* Check For E-mail *or* Check Mail *or* Refresh Mail	Check the Inbox for new messages.
Create Mail *or* Create New Mail *or* New Mail *or* New E-mail *or* New Message	Create a new e-mail message.
Open Mail *or* Open E-mail *or* Open That	Open the selected e-mail message.
Close Mail *or* Close E-mail *or* Close That	Close the selected e-mail message window. This command does not close your main e-mail program. It does not work in Netscape Messenger.

TIP *You can say "Mail," "E-mail," "Message," or "Memo" in any of the commands specific to e-mail.*

The following commands work if you have a message selected in your Inbox, or if you are currently in an e-mail message.

Sending, replying to, forwarding, and printing e-mail

SAY	TO
Reply Mail *or* Reply Message *or* Reply To E-Mail *or* Reply To Message	Reply to the sender of the current message.
Reply to All	Reply to all recipients of the current message.
Forward Mail *or* Forward E-Mail *or* Forward Message	Forward the current message.
Send Mail *or* Send E-Mail *or* Send Message	Sends the current message.
Send Now *or* Send Mail Now	**In AOL only**, sends the current message immediately.
Send Later *or* Send Mail Later	**In AOL only**, sends the current message later.
Print Mail *or* Print E-Mail *or* Print Message	Prints the current message.
Delete Mail *or* Delete E-Mail *or* Delete Message	Deletes the current message.

The following commands let you move around when editing e-mail. You can also use the regular text editing commands to compose your messages.

NOTE *You cannot use e-mail commands when editing mail in the Word editor started by Outlook. In Outlook 2000, you select the Word editor on the Mail Format tab of the Options dialog box, which you open using the the Options command on the Tools menu. Outlook uses the Word editor for messages if you select Use Microsoft Word to edit email messages and you set the message format to HTML or plain text. Also, make sure the option to Allow Natural Language Commands in Microsoft Word (on the Startup/ Shutdown tab of the Options dialog box) is not selected.*

Editing a message

SAY	TO
Go to To Field *or* To	Move to the To field. **In AOL only**, you can say "Send To."
Go to CC Field *or* CC	Move to the CC field. **In AOL only**, you can say "Copy To."
Go to BCC Field *or* BCC	Move to the BCC field.
Go to Subject Field Subject	Move to the Subject field.
Go to Body Field *or* Body	Move to the Body field.
Go To First Field *or* First	Move to the first field of the view.
Go To Next Field *or* Next	Move to the next field of the view.
Go To Previous Field *or* Previous	Move to the previous field of the view.
Go To Last Field *or* Last	Move to the last field of the view.

TIP *You can also say "Move To" instead of "Go To" in any of the commands above.*

Using Lotus Notes

Lotus Notes commands are available only in Dragon NaturallySpeaking Professional and higher editions. These commands let you control and navigate using Lotus Notes.

Basic commands

SAY	TO
Move to Tab *1..10*	Move to the selected Lotus Notes tab.
Next Message	Open the next message in the list.
Previous Message	Open the previous message in the list.
Next Unread	Open the next unread message.
Open Document	Open the selected document.
Close Document	Close the selected document.
Open *By Category*	Open the view named *By Category*.
Show Me My *Calendar*	Open the view named *Calendar*.
Click *Move to Folder*	Click the toolbar button named *Move to Folder*.
What Field Is This	Display the Notes Field ID.
Format That	Display the text properties dialog for selected text in a Notes document.
Refresh View	Update the view.

TIP *You can say "Move To" or "Go To" the name of any Notes field, such as "Move To Home Phone" in your address book to go to the Home Phone field.*

You can also use Dragon NaturallySpeaking e-mail commands when composing e-mail in Lotus Notes. Use the standard Dragon NaturallySpeaking editing commands to work with text that you enter.

NOTE *You cannot select paragraphs in Lotus Notes, or format text using the Set Font and Format That commands described in the section on "Formatting text" on page 98.*

For more information about Lotus Notes, see the online Help.

Using Internet Explorer

These commands are fully supported in Internet Explorer 5, though most are available in Internet Explorer 4.

Navigating the Web

SAY	TO
Go to Address	Move to the Address box.
Click Go *or* Go There	Go to the Web page specified in the Address box (same as pressing the ENTER key).
Go to Favorite *Dragon Systems*	Go to a Web page on your Favorites list, in this example, *Dragon Systems*.
Refresh *or* Reload	Refresh the current Web page (same as clicking the Refresh button).
Click *Help on Searching* or *Help on Searching*	Follow the link or click the button, in this example, *Help on Searching*.
Click *About Dragon* or *About Dragon*	Follow the link that appears in an image when the mouse moves over it, in this example, *About Dragon*.
Choose *2*	Select an alternative from the numbered list and enter it in your document. You can say any number that appears in the list.
Next Match *or* Next	Select the next matching link or object on the page.
Previous Match *or* Previous	Select the previous matching link or object on the page.
Click That *or* That One	Click the selected link, edit box, and so on.
Stop Loading	Stop loading a Web page (same as clicking the Stop button).
Go Back	Load the previous Web page in your history list (same as clicking the Back button).
Go Forward	Load the next Web page in your history list (same as clicking the Forward button).
Go Home	Go to your home page (same as clicking the Home button).

Moving around a Web page

SAY	TO
Page Down	Scroll down one screen (same as pressing the PAGE DOWN key).
Page Up	Scroll up one screen (same as pressing the PAGE UP key).
Line Down	Scroll down one line (same as clicking the down arrow in the scroll bar once).
Line Up	Scroll up one line (same as clicking the up arrow in the scroll bar once).
Go to Top	Scroll to the beginning of the Web page.
Go to Bottom	Scroll to the end of the Web page.
Start Scrolling Down	Start automatic scrolling toward the end of the page.
Start Scrolling Up	Start automatic scrolling toward the beginning of the page.
Stop Scrolling	Stop automatic scrolling.
Speed Up	Increase scrolling speed. (Say it again to speed up more.)
Slow Down	Decrease scrolling speed. (Say it again to slow down more.)
Next Frame	Go to the next frame in a multiframe page.
Previous Frame	Go to the previous frame in a multiframe page.

Working with forms

SAY	TO
Type Text *or* Edit Box	Go to the first place on a Web page you can enter text.
Click Check Box *or* Check Box	Enumerate all check boxes on the page, and go to the first one.
Click Image *or* Image	Enumerate all images with links on the page, and go to the first one.
Choose *2*	Select the image, option, button, and so on from the enumerated list of choices. You can say any number that appears in the list.

SAY	TO
Click Radio Button/ Radio Button	Enumerate all option (radio) buttons on the page, and go to the first one.
Click List Box *or* List Box	Enumerate all the boxes with a list of choices (drop-down lists) on the page, and go to the first one.
Show Choices	Open a list of choices.
Hide Choices	Close a list of choices.
Cancel Choices	Deactivates a list of choices, leaving the most recent choice selected.
Choose *Thursday* or *Thursday*	Chooses an entry from a list of choices, in this example, *Thursday*.

You can use standard editing commands to work with text that you enter in a Web form.

For more information about Internet Explorer commands, see "Working with Internet Explorer" on page 123.

Working hands-free

Pressing keyboard keys
For lists of commands you can use to press keyboard keys, see "Pressing keyboard keys" on page 111.

Moving the mouse pointer and clicking the mouse
For lists of commands you can use to move the mouse pointer and click the mouse, see "Moving the mouse pointer and clicking the mouse" on page 115.

Index

W
Wake Up   173
Web addresses   72, 124
Web pages. *See* Internet Explorer
What's new in version 5   2
windows
   closing   110, 199
   resizing   110, 199
   switching between   106
Windows Explorer   104
Windows NT   103
WordPad   172
WordPerfect   46, 87, 98, 171–172
words
   deleting   94, 101–102
   moving to next/previous   90
   placing insertion point before/after   88
   selecting   92, 94
WorldWide Web. *See* Internet Explorer
written forms   39, 42

Y
years   79

Z
Zip codes   85

DRAGON SYSTEMS USA

A Lernout & Hauspie Company
320 Nevada Street
Newton, Massachusetts 02460
USA

Tel: +1-617-965-5200
Fax: +1-617-527-0372
E-mail: info@dragonsys.com

Web: www.dragonsystems.com

DRAGON SYSTEMS UK

A Lernout & Hauspie Company
Seagate House
Globe Park
Marlow
Buckinghamshire SL7 1LW
United Kingdom

Tel: +44 (0) 1628 894150
Fax: +44 (0) 1628 894151
E-mail: info@dragon.co.uk

WORLDWIDE HEADQUARTERS

Lernout & Hauspie Speech Products N.V.
Flanders Languages Valley, 50
8900 Ieper Belgium

Tel: +32-57-228-888
Fax: +32-57-208-48

Web: www.LHSL.com